Valuing Natural Capital

Future Proofing Business and Finance

GW00645233

Dorothy Maxwell

DMaxwell@SustBusinessGroup.com

www.dorothymaxwell.com

@DrDMaxwell

First published in 2015 by Dō Sustainability

87 Lonsdale Road, Oxford OX2 7ET, UK

Copyright © 2015 Dorothy Maxwell

The moral right of the author has been asserted.

All rights reserved. No part of this publication may be reproduced, stored in a retrieval system, or transmitted, in any form or by any means, electronic, mechanical, photocopying, recording or otherwise, except as expressly permitted by law, without the prior, written permission of the publisher.

ISBN 978-1-910174-45-6 (eBook-ePub)

ISBN 978-1-910174-46-3 (eBook-PDF)

ISBN 978-1-910174-44-9 (Paperback)

A catalogue record for this title is available from the British Library.

Dō Sustainability strives for net positive social and environmental impact. See our sustainability policy at **www.dosustainability.com**.

Page design and typesetting by Alison Rayner

Cover by Becky Chilcott

For further information on Dō Sustainability, visit our website: **www.dosustainability.com**

DōShorts

Dō Sustainability is the publisher of **DōShorts**: short, high-value business guides that distill sustainability best practice and business insights for busy, results-driven professionals. Each DōShort can be read in 90 minutes.

New and forthcoming DōShorts – stay up to date

We publish new DōShorts each month. The best way to keep up to date? Sign up to our short, monthly newsletter. Go to **www.dosustainability. com/newsletter** to sign up to the Dō Newsletter. Some of our latest and forthcoming titles include:

- *Making Sustainability Matter: How To Make Materiality Drive Profit, Strategy and Communications*   Dwayne Baraka
- *Creating a Sustainable Brand: A Guide to Growing the Sustainability Top Line*   Henk Campher
- *Cultivating System Change: A Practitioner's Companion*   Anna Birney
- *How Much Energy Does Your Building Use?*   Liz Reason
- *Lobbying for Good: How Business Advocacy Can Accelerate the Delivery of a Sustainable Economy*   Paul Monaghan & Philip Monaghan
- *Creating Employee Champions: How to Drive Business Success Through Sustainability Engagement Training*   Joanna M. Sullivan
- *Smart Engagement: Why, What, Who and How*   John Aston & Alan Knight
- *How to Produce a Sustainability Report*   Kye Gbangbola & Nicole Lawler

- *Strategic Sustainable Procurement: An Overview of Law and Best Practice for the Public and Private Sectors* Colleen Theron & Malcolm Dowden

- *The Reputation Risk Handbook: Surviving and Thriving in the Age of Hyper-Transparency* Andrea Bonime-Blanc

- *Business Strategy for Water Challenges: From Risk to Opportunity* Stuart Orr and Guy Pegram

- *Accelerating Sustainability Using the 80/20 Rule* Gareth Kane

- *The Guide to the Circular Economy: Capturing Value and Managing Material Risk* Dustin Benton, Jonny Hazell and Julie Hill

- *PR 2.0: How Digital Media Can Help You Build a Sustainable Brand* John Friedman

Subscriptions

In addition to individual sales of our ebooks, we now offer subscriptions. Access 60+ ebooks for the price of 6 with a personal subscription to our full e-library. Institutional subscriptions are also available for your staff or students. Visit **www.dosustainability.com/books/subscriptions** or email **veruschka@dosustainability.com**

Write for us, or suggest a DōShort

Please visit **www.dosustainability.com** for our full publishing programme. If you don't find what you need, write for us! Or suggest a DōShort on our website. We look forward to hearing from you.

Abstract

NATURAL CAPITAL – the resources and services nature provides – are key factors underpinning our global economy. While the long-term viability of business and society depends on maintaining this natural capital, many forms such as freshwater, forests and biodiversity are being consumed at an alarming rate. What's more, critical support systems such as the ability to regulate climate, are failing. This is because natural capital's many benefits are taken for granted and assumed to be free, despite their vast social and economic value. The future shock for business is the potential for profit to be wiped out as natural capital is internalized through regulation and markets. As sustainability challenges continue to escalate, businesses and their investors need to understand their natural capital risks and opportunities alongside their financial impacts. Finance provides a common language vital to communicating trade-offs and prioritizing sustainability at CFO, CEO and board level. Furthermore, as natural capital's costs and benefits impact society, it is inextricably linked with social and other forms of capital. Companies who act now to future-proof themselves are best positioned to manage and thrive in a resource-constrained world. They will mitigate risk, secure their resource supplies, create long-term value and enhance their, resilience, reputation and competitive advantage. To succeed, they must integrate natural and social capital in the business model. This book provides a succinct introduction to natural capital, its links to social and other capitals and how to use it to support better decision-making in business. Views from natural capital leaders across business, finance, accounting,

government, research and NGO communities illustrate the theory with practice. Quotes and case examples from senior executives (CFO, CEO and Heads of Sustainability) in early adopter businesses (Kingfisher Group, Dow Chemical Company, The Crown Estate, Patagonia®, United Utilities and Marks & Spencer) and Financial Institutions (Inter-American Development Bank (IDB), Citi Group and Credit Suisse) show the way.
....

About the Author

Photo courtesy of
Brian Minehane
....

DR DOROTHY MAXWELL (www.dorothymaxwell.com) has been working in sustainability with businesses, government and NGOs for 24 years in the USA, Europe and Asia Pacific. She has a PhD in Environmental Science and Masters in Environmental Economics & Law. She specializes in sustainability in business. She has worked with Accenture and Willis risk management, was Director of the Irish government Sustainable Business Programme (**www.envirocentre.ie/index.html**) and an environmental policy-maker with the European Commission and United Nations Environment Programme. Since 2006, she is the Founding Director of The Sustainable Business Group (previously Global View Sustainability Services; **www.SustBusinessGroup.com**) consultancy whose clients include Wal-Mart, Nike, the UK Department of the Environment, Food and Rural Affairs (DEFRA) and European Commission. She has been Special Advisor to The Prince of Wales's International Sustainability Unit (**www.pcfisu.org**) and DEFRA's Sustainable Products and Green Economy programmes (2006–10) (**https://www.gov.uk/government/policies/encouraging-businesses-to-manage-their-impact-on-the-environment**). She was the founding Executive Director of the Natural Capital Coalition (2012–14) (**www.naturalcapitalcoalition.org**) (and author of their 2014 *Valuing Nature in Business* (**www.thesustainablebusinessgroup.com**). She is a lecturer on sustainable business at the Imperial College London (**www3.imperial.ac.uk/environmentalpolicy/teaching/msc**).

A passionate advocate about the need for clear business communication on what can be complex sustainability topics, she speaks at events and has authored multiple publications. More information is at **www. dorothymaxwell.com** and **www.SustBusinessGroup.com.**

Acknowledgments

I EXTEND MY SINCERE THANKS to those who generously gave their time and expertise to inform this publication. You have brought my words to life with your rich experiences across business and finance.

Foreword: Sir Ian Cheshire, former Group CEO Kingfisher, plc

Reviewers:

Chartered Institute of Management Accountants, Sandra Rapacioli, Head of Sustainability Research and Policy

Corporate Eco Forum, PJ Simmons, Chair and Co-Founder

Case examples:

The Dow Chemical Company, Mark Weick, Director, Sustainability Programs and Enterprise Risk Management

The Crown Estate, Alison Nimmo, CEO; John Lelliott, Finance Director; Mark Gough, Head of Sustainability

Marks & Spencer, Adam Elman, Head of Global Plan A Delivery

Otto Group, Dr Johannes Merck, VP Sustainability, Stephan Engel and Dr Moritz Nils, Systain

Patagonia, Rick Ridgeway, VP

United Utilities Group PLC, Russ Houlden, CFO

ACKNOWLEDGMENTS

Views and quotes:

ACCA, Rachel Jackson, Head of Sustainability

The Prince's Accounting for Sustainability Project, Jessica Fries, Executive Chairman

The Aldersgate Group, Peter Young, Chairman

Bloomberg LP, Andrew Park, Head of Sustainable Finance Programs

Business for Social Responsibility, Aron Cramer, President and CEO

Carbon Disclosure Standards Board, Mardi O'Brien, CEO

Citi, Courtney Lowrance, Director, Environmental and Social Risk Management

Credit Suisse AG, Ben Ridley, Sustainability Affairs, Asia Pacific

Department of the Environment Food and Rural Affairs, Helen Dunn, Senior Economic Advisor

EY, Steven Lang, Partner

The Generation Foundation, Generation Investment Management, Daniela Saltzman, Director

Green Economy Coalition, Oliver Greenfield, Convenor

International Federation of Accountants, Stathis Gould, Head of Professional Accountants in Business

Inter-American Development Bank, Hans Schulz, Vice President for the Private Sector and Non-Sovereign Guaranteed Operations

International Integrated Reporting Council, Paul Druckman, CEO

The Nature Conservancy, Mark Tercek, President

University of East Anglia, Prof. Tim O'Riordan OBE DL FBA, Emeritus Professor of Environmental Sciences

University of Technology Sydney, Rosemary Sainty

WWF-UK, Stuart Poore, Director of Corporate Sustainability

My sincere thanks to Dr Nick Bellorini, Publishing Director and Dō Sustainability colleagues

To Brian, without your limitless support and encouragement this book would not have happened!

To my father, thank you for inspiring me to write.

Contents

3 Drivers and Current Context..............79

4 Challenges, Opportunities and Next Steps..............97

Foreword
Sir Ian Cheshire,
former Group CEO, Kingfisher plc

Photo courtesy of
Kingfisher plc

MOST BUSINESSES DON'T REALLY UNDERSTAND how they depend on natural and social capital. We all understand financial capital, the profit and loss (P&L) and balance sheet, but there is a much bigger picture, which business is just beginning to appreciate. It is that everything we do as businesses depends on society and nature creating the conditions for us to succeed. While we may take these gifts for granted and assume they will continue to be free forever, the world is now changing. As a result, our business models are under threat, but for the 'leadership' businesses this shift will also bring new opportunities. Dr Maxwell brings this issue into focus with a practical guide to current thinking and a call to action that CEOs should heed.

This change in the world around us is happening as a result of shifts in commodity costs, consumer and political awareness, but especially because it is now clear that our current economic system doesn't adequately capture the real picture of the costs to the world of our operations. If you think water will continue to be nearly free, if timber will be available at current prices for ever, if waste is a zero cost issue, then your business model will be obsolete in less than ten years. The externalities will be priced in one way or another.

What business needs to help embrace this change are two key shifts: first, as Dr Maxwell describes, a truly inclusive accounting framework that gives us the fully integrated picture of our businesses and allow us to value non-financial factors. This is no small challenge given we have over 700 years of practice with double-entry bookkeeping and almost none in Triple Net Bottom Line (TNBL) analysis.

Second, we need our investors and financiers to value businesses differently as a result of these new analytical tools. It cannot be right that an exploitative short-term model is given the same price-to-earnings (P/E) ratio as a business capable of lasting for 50 years and positively impacting the planet as it makes money.

Dr Maxwell's book is a really important contribution to a vital topic that businesses need to understand, and especially for the CEOs who are charged with the longer-term stewardship of their firms. The future may be challenging but also filled with opportunity for those who truly understand the natural capital context in which they operate. Good luck to those pioneers!

*Sir Ian Cheshire is the former Group CEO of Kingfisher plc. (**www. kingfisher.com**), the largest home improvement retailer in Europe and third largest in the world. With Kingfisher for 17 years, Sir Ian has been the CEO of B&Q and CEO of the Group since 2008. He is one of the first CEOs to explicitly link sustainability performance with business opportunity. His leadership and passion for sustainable innovation have created a strong legacy including spearheading the development of the Forest Stewardship*

Council (*www.ic.fcs.org*), One Planet Living and pioneering restorative business approach Net Positive (*www.kingfisher.com/netpositive/index. asp?pageid=1*). He has taken Kingfisher on a transformative journey that demonstrates that business can grow stronger and profitable, while make a positive contribution to people and planet. He has been the chair of the UK government's Ecosystems Market Task Force (*https://www.gov.uk/government/groups/ecosystem-markets-task-force#role-of-the-group*), won The Guardian Sustainable Business Leader of the Year award and was knighted in 2014 for services to business, sustainability and the environment.

....

Who Is This Book For?

THIS BOOK IS INTENDED for corporations, financial institutions and professional services supporting them. It is suitable for C-suite (CEO, CFO and Head of Sustainability) as well as operational levels including accountants and other practitioners (sustainability and financial related). This is a must-read for sectors with high natural capital dependencies including food, extractives, energy, water utilities, timber and, on a cross-cutting basis, finance. It will also be of general interest across all business sectors.

It will clarify 1) what natural capital is, its links to social and other capitals and the state of play; 2) the business case for using it in decision-making, 3) where natural capital accounting and valuation fits in the current sustainability and financial toolbox; and 4) what real life early adopters in business are doing. Written in language suited to business professionals it will cut through the sustainability jargon and provide the 'need to know' facts.

Business is defined to be corporations operating in different sectors and financial institutions, for example, banking, pensions, insurance and accounting.

Terms used are included in the glossary on page 111.

The table below offers some guidance for the following audiences:

IF YOU ARE:	THIS BOOK WILL HELP YOU:
CFO and executives	Understand the commercial rationale for integrating natural and social capital considerations in management and financial accounting/reporting to inform assessment of risk and opportunities.
Head of Sustainability	Embed the latest thinking on natural and social capital into the business sustainability strategy and management.
Investor	Understand the rationale for integrating natural and social capital considerations in Environmental, Social and Governance assessment of investments.
Sustainability professional	Embed natural and social capital into sustainable business measurement, management and reporting.
Accountant or finance professional	Why and how to embed natural and social capital in management and financial accounting/reporting.

PART 1

Business Case

Future-proofing against natural capital shocks

NATURAL CAPITAL – the critical systems and resources nature provides – underpins the successful functioning of our economy, businesses and societal wellbeing. However, much of this capital, for example, freshwater, forests and biodiversity are being depleted at an alarming rate and critical support systems such as the ability to regulate climate and flood defences are failing. The social and economic value of natural

FIGURE 1. Comparison of global GDP, economic value of natures services and costs to maintain (per annum).

USD$63 Trillion   USD$50 Trillion   USD$93 Billion

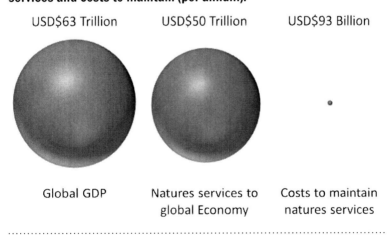

Global GDP   Natures services to global Economy   Costs to maintain natures services

capital is vast, yet it is not adequately captured in the market. According to the Chartered Institute of Management Accounting (CIMA) and EY, 'Natural Capital is the Elephant in the Boardroom – it is invisible in the vast majority of corporate decisions, accounts and economic models.'[1] This is one of the causes of its ongoing degradation.

As illustrated in Figure 1, very conservative estimates of economic value provided by nature's services to the global economy are $US50 trillion/year compared to global GDP $US63 trillion/year. In comparison, a relatively small $93 billion is estimated as needed to preserve natural capital (figures are for 2010).[2] This puts the scale in context.

Examples of economic values estimated for a selection of nature's services is in Figure 2.

FIGURE 2. Estimated market values for a sample of nature's services (base years vary).[3]

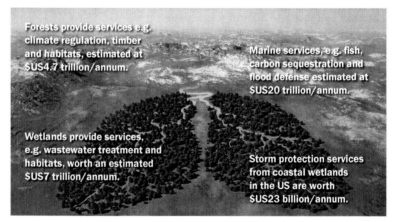

Forests provide services e.g. climate regulation, timber and habitats, estimated at $US4.7 trillion/annum.

Marine services, e.g. fish, carbon sequestration and flood defense estimated at $US20 trillion/annum.

Wetlands provide services, e.g. wastewater treatment and habitats, worth an estimated $US7 trillion/annum.

Storm protection services from coastal wetlands in the US are worth $US23 billion/annum.

SOURCE: Image from Shutterstock, used under standard Content Usage Agreement

The global cost of environmental damage from business activities such as water pollution, loss of fertile land, soil erosion, drought, overfishing and deforestation is estimated at over $US6 trillion.[4] This is estimated to rise to $US28 trillion by 2050[5] if 'business as usual' continues. If Mother Nature sent an invoice, estimates for the cost of the top 100 environmental externalities from business to the global economy/annum are over $US4 trillion according to a study from the Natural Capital Coalition.[6] This includes costs from GHG emissions, pollution, land conversion, waste and water use from primary business sectors across world regions. The top 20 sectors with highest costs and regions most impacted are illustrated in Figure 3.

FIGURE 3. Ranking of the top 20 sectors and regions with the highest natural capital cost. The largest impact is noted.

RANK	IMPACT	SECTOR	REGION	NATURAL CAPITAL COST, US$ BN	REVENUE, US$ BN
1	GHG	COAL POWER GENERATION	EASTERN ASIA	361.0	443.1
2	LAND USE	CATTLE RANCHING AND FARMING	SOUTH AMERICA	312.1	16.6
3	GHG	IRON AND STEEL MILLS	EASTERN ASIA	216.1	604.7
4	WATER	WHEAT FARMING	SOUTHERN ASIA	214.4	31.8
5	GHG	COAL POWER GENERATION	NORTHERN AMERICA	201.0	246.7
6	GHG	CEMENT MANUFACTURING	EASTERN ASIA	139.9	174.0
7	LAND USE	CATTLE RANCHING AND FARMING	SOUTHERN ASIA	131.4	5.8
8	WATER	RICE FARMING	SOUTHERN ASIA	123.7	65.8
9	AIR POLLUTANTS	COAL POWER GENERATION	NORTHERN AMERICA	113.4	246.7
10	WATER	WATER SUPPLY	SOUTHERN ASIA	92.0	14.1
11	WATER	WHEAT FARMING	NORTHERN AFRICA	89.6	7.4
12	AIR POLLUTANTS	COAL POWER GENERATION	EASTERN ASIA	88.3	443.1
13	WATER	RICE FARMING	NORTHERN AFRICA	82.3	1.2
14	LAND USE	RICE FARMING	SOUTHERN ASIA	81.8	65.8
15	WATER	WATER SUPPLY	WESTERN ASIA	81.7	18.4
16	LAND USE	FISHING	GLOBAL	80.0	136.0
17	WATER	CORN FARMING	NORTHERN AFRICA	79.3	1.7
18	WATER	WATER SUPPLY	NORTHERN AFRICA	73.7	3.4
19	GHG	PETROLEUM AND NATURAL GAS EXTRACTION	EASTERN EUROPE	71.6	371.6
20	WATER	SUGARCANE	SOUTHERN ASIA	63.3	6.0

SOURCE: Natural Capital at Risk – Top 100 Externalities of Business, p. 28. Copyright © Trucost for Natural Capital Coalition (**www.naturalcapitalcoalition.org**), 15 April 2013

The study estimated that the profits of many high impact sectors would be wiped out if these costs were accounted for. While there are many assumptions and uncertainties built into the calculations of these costs, the important message is the urgent financial rationale for reducing natural capital risk. If these externalities were internalized through regulation, taxation or markets, many sectors annual profits would not cover the bill.

The future shock for business is the potential for profit to be wiped out as natural capital is internalized through regulation, taxation and markets. Companies who act now to future-proof are better positioned to manage and thrive in a future 'resource-constrained' world.

Our current economic and business models assume an infinite supply of natural resources and functioning ecosystems. This is flawed. One of the main drivers for integrating natural capital considerations in business is to understand the risks and opportunities from growing resource scarcity, malfunctioning ecosystems and increasingly erratic weather events associated with climate change. This is particularly the case for sectors with high natural capital dependencies, for example, food, energy generation, extractives, forestry, water utilities, pharmaceuticals and tourism.[7] For example, an estimated 25–50 percent of the pharmaceutical market is derived from nature's genetic diversity.[8] It is estimated the Earth is losing one major drug every two years due to natural capital degradation.[9] The Corporate Eco Forum (**www.corporateecoforum.com/valuing-natural-capital-initiative/**) describes the backlog of debt this stripping of assets is causing:

A new kind of global debt crisis is brewing—this time, due to decades of over-borrowing from our planet's natural capital asset base. At risk are critical life-support systems that are also the lifeblood of our global economy. Farsighted business leaders grasp what's at stake. They see the business logic in taking action today – both to avert tomorrow's on-balance-sheet risks, as well as to seize new revenue opportunities available to companies that generate environmentally restorative solutions.

P.J. SIMMONS, CO-FOUNDER AND CHAIR, CORPORATE ECO FORUM

Business case for corporations

Measuring the environmental and social impacts of businesses is largely mainstream. Measuring its dependencies on natural capital stocks and services is not. Measuring both impacts and dependencies gives a holistic picture of risks and opportunities. *Financially valuing* these further translates this 'non–financial' information into 'financial'. This common language can play an important role in communicating and prioritizing sustainability at the CFO and board level. It can enable the most significant or *'material'* (in financial accounting language) to be understood in commercial terms and the implications for the company and its wider business model.

> **Materiality** – issues that substantively affect the organization's ability to create value over the short, medium and long term.[10]

For a corporation, delaying the measurement and management of natural capital carries a significant business risk for availability of key raw materials,

Valuing impacts and dependencies in financial terms translates 'non-financial' information into 'financial' information. This common language plays an important role in communicating and prioritizing sustainability at the CFO and board level.

associated price volatility and maintaining competitive advantage. For example, by analysing natural resource risk, associated price volatility and other sustainability improvements implemented, Unilever (www.unilever.com/images/PDF_generator_-_Greenhouse_gases _tcm_13-365028.pdf) estimates savings of €300 million ($US370 million) in avoided costs since 2008 (figures for 2012).[11] On the positive side, financial valuation of natural capital costs and benefits also informs decisions on capital allocation, new investments, market opportunities and return on investment. For example, The Dow Chemical Company (Dow) integration of financial valuation of wetland services identified *Net Present Value* (NPV) savings of $US282 million for implementing a constructed wetland instead of an effluent treatment plant over the project's lifetime, plus a wide range of non-financial biodiversity benefits. The UK's largest property and landowner, The Crown Estate determined their Windsor Estate delivers £4.4 million ($US6.6 million) per annum gross external benefit using their Total Contribution approach to measure their environmental, social and economic value. More generally, measuring the costs and benefits of sustainability in business demonstrate their financial business case. Marks and Spencer (M&S) have shown their Plan A (now Plan A 2020) sustainability programme has delivered financial savings of £465 million ($US701million) plus wider benefits including staff motivation, brand enhancement and supply chain resiliency over the seven years it has been operating (see The Crown Estate, Dow and M&S case examples in Chapter 2).

A survey of 26 business early adopters on natural capital[12] identified their rationale for early action as being much better positioned than other companies to manage and thrive in a future 'resource-constrained world'. First mover advantage has also been a motivation, for example, PUMA's (part of Kering Group; www.kering.com/en/sustainability/environmental-pl) early leadership example of an Environmental Profit & Loss account monetizing their environmental impacts across the supply chain.[13]

Several business case rationales from early adopters are described.

Dow believes that valuing nature makes good business sense. Valuing natural capital and ecosystem services helps Dow make better business decisions for Dow, for our communities, and for the planet we share. MARK WEICK, DIRECTOR, SUSTAINABILITY PROGRAMS AND ENTERPRISE RISK MANAGEMENT, THE DOW CHEMICAL COMPANY

Sustainability is both a moral and commercial imperative – in short, there is a business case for going green. ADAM ELMAN, GLOBAL HEAD OF DELIVERY – PLAN A, MARKS & SPENCER PLC

For me sustainability is a central driving factor behind our strategy and our long-term commercial success. Total Contribution has helped us to take a more rounded look at how we measure the value this creates – going beyond just the numbers and fulfilling the old adage, we treasure what we measure. ALISON NIMMO, CEO, THE CROWN ESTATE

Of course, the bounty of nature is priceless. But the unfortunate effect of our seeing these inputs to well-being as incalculable has been that they are treated as free. That mind-set creates problems when resources turn out not to be limitless or indestructible. A failure to price resources also makes it difficult to think clearly about trade-offs, which many decisions relating to sustainability involve. When inputs and outputs can be stated in like terms (which is to say, dollar terms), optimal solutions can be found. YVON CHOUINARD, ROCK CLIMBER, FOUNDER AND CHAIRMAN, PATAGONIA®, RICK RIDGEWAY, MOUNTAINEER, VP PATAGONIA® AND RESPONSIBLE FOR ENVIRONMENTAL INITIATIVES, JIB ELLISON, FOUNDER AND CEO BLU SKYE – THE BIG IDEA, THE SUSTAINABLE ECONOMY[14]

Business case for financial institutions

Regarding investor interests, at a big picture level, the evidence base for sustainability driving financial performance through lower cost of capital, better operational performance or improved stock price is growing.[15],[16] For example, the Arabesque Asset Management and University of Oxford's 2014 report *From the Stockholder to the Stakeholder: How sustainability can drive financial outperformance* showed a strong correlation between improved financial and investment performance as sustainable business practice improves.[17] The study concludes: 'When investors and asset owners replace the question "how much return?" with "how much sustainable return?", then they have evolved from a stockholder to a stakeholder.'[18] A Harvard Business School and the London Business School meta-study of 180 previous studies showed that high sustainability performing companies outperformed low performers in the stock market over an 18-year period.[19] For financial institutions, the business case for integrating natural and social capital in investment decisions is that it informs assessment of material risks and opportunities in terms of assets and liabilities. This can be applied in Environmental, Social and Governance (ESG) assessments for companies and across investment portfolios to give a more informed view of sustainability performance. It can also inform equities research and development of new financial products.

From a risk perspective, identifying the potential for *Stranded Assets* in investment decisions is a particular priority in light of sustainability challenges. This can cause significant reductions in the long-term value of entire sectors and companies, for example, fossil fuel-based energy generation, food and pharmaceuticals.

> **Stranded Asset** – an asset which loses significant economic value well ahead of its anticipated useful life as a result of changes in legislation, regulation, market forces, disruptive innovation, societal norms or environmental shocks.

Stranded Assets associated with carbon-intensive industries is one example of how financial valuation informs investors. In light of the transition to a low carbon economy, climate change regulation and carbon pricing, investors need to understand the vulnerability of conventional assets caused by stranding. As one example, Bloomberg's Carbon Risk Valuation Tool[20] aims to assess the implications of stranding on a company's earnings and share price.

As water scarcity becomes the next growing risk, Bloomberg LP's perspective is:

Operating in water-stressed locations can pose financial risks in many industries. Traditional financial analysis does not, however, typically account for outcomes such as shutdowns, regulatory penalties or unplanned capital expenditures linked to water stress. Bloomberg LP, together with the Natural Capital Declaration (www.naturalcapitaldeclaration.org), has developed a flexible, first generation quantitative tool to demonstrate how water can potentially impact a company's valuation using familiar analytical approaches. ANDREW PARK, SUSTAINABLE FINANCE, BLOOMBERG LP

Interest in natural and social capital risk is growing in banks, pension funds, investors and insurers. Business case rationales from early adopter financial institutions are described.

Accounting for natural capital in project decisions is becoming increasingly important for our clients as well as for our own financing decisions. Citi has led key initiatives including The Biodiversity for Banks (B4B)[21] program to help banks incorporate the value of nature into their lending decisions and client engagements. COURTNEY LOWRANCE, DIRECTOR, ENVIRONMENTAL AND SOCIAL RISK MANAGEMENT, CITI

Credit Suisse are actively engaged in helping banks better understand the full value of natural capital through supporting emerging initiatives, for example, the WWF ESG in Banking Guide[22] and co-authorship, with WWF and McKinsey, of a conservation finance research paper.[23] Ben Ridley, Head of Sustainability Affairs Asia Pacific explains the business case for banks to integrate natural capital in investment:

Natural capital underpins the value chains from which financial wealth is generated, but accounting for major adverse impacts on natural capital, and/or upon communities that rely on it, is a work in progress. Parallel efforts to redefine materiality are underway in many global financial institutions too, as evidenced by ESG integration in equity research and in the development of financial products and services. BEN RIDLEY, HEAD OF SUSTAINABILITY AFFAIRS, ASIA PACIFIC, CREDIT SUISSE AG

Development banks have an added driver for strong sustainability performance given their mandate to support long-term development. FMO, the Dutch Development Bank (**www.fmo.nl/sustain ability2**) and Inter-American Development Bank (IDB; **www.iadb. org/en/topics/environment/biodiversity-platform/the-idbs-biodiversity-platform,6825.html**) are examples of innovative early adopters on natural capital. IDB invests in the Latin America and Caribbean (LAC) region. The LAC region is among the richest in the world in biological diversity[24] – a web of life that provides countless benefits vital to human life and LAC's economies. As the region's populations and economies expand, so do opportunities for investing in this valuable asset. Wisely managed, biodiversity and ecosystem services hold significant promise for long-term growth and prosperity. To help fulfil this promise, IDB developed the Biodiversity and Ecosystems Services Program to help maintain LAC's remarkable biodiversity and ecosystems while driving economic growth and contributing to wellbeing for all. Hans Schulz,

Vice President for the Private Sector and Non-Sovereign Guaranteed Operations, IDB describes their business case rationale:

In a uniquely bio-diverse region, Latin America and the Caribbean's natural capital plays a critical role in supporting people and businesses. The Biodiversity and Ecosystems Services Program is an integral part of our strategy that allows us to increase lending for green investments. Assessing client dependency on ecosystem services and using market studies to explore new sectors, we are building the business case for investing in natural capital. Working in LAC, where the economy depends especially on agriculture, we've focused our efforts to show that improved management of ecosystem services in agribusiness can increase harvest quantity and quality. HANS SCHULZ, VICE PRESIDENT FOR THE PRIVATE SECTOR AND NON-SOVEREIGN GUARANTEED OPERATIONS, IDB

The business case for integrating natural and social capital is clear for reasons of risk mitigation, securing resource supply, resilience, maintaining a licence to operate, reputation, profitability and long-term value creation. As outlined in Chapter 3, pricing and other market incentives are coming. National accounting systems to support 'Beyond GDP/GNP' metrics are underway in many countries. This will enable future policy tools, for example, natural asset pricing, resources targets and taxation, to be developed. New markets driving carbon reductions, conservation of biodiversity, water, forests and sustainable investment are growing opportunities. The increasing number of country's requiring mandatory sustainability reporting is a further driver for increasing financial and non-financial accountability. Overall, companies that get ahead will come out ahead, those that do not will fall behind and may not survive. From The Nature Conservancy (**www.nature.org/science-in-action/ecosystem-services.xml**) perspective:

> *Forward-thinking business leaders know that investing in nature isn't just the right thing to do – it's the smart thing to do. These leaders understand the value of nature that sustains industries: the oceans that provide seafood; the forests that protect watersheds and arable land; the healthy soils that grow crops; the rivers that provide fresh water; the coastal ecosystems that provide protection from storms and sea level rise. Investing in the long-term health of these resources can help companies manage risks to their supply chains, keep costs down, identify new market opportunities, and protect essential business assets.*
>
> MARK R. TERCEK, PRESIDENT AND CEO, THE NATURE CONSERVANCY, AND AUTHOR OF *NATURE'S FORTUNE: HOW BUSINESS AND SOCIETY THRIVE BY INVESTING IN NATURE (www.marktercek.com/natures-fortune/)*

The business case for integrating natural and social capital is growing for reasons of risk mitigation, securing resource supply, resilience, maintaining a licence to operate, reputation, profitability and long-term value creation.

Natural capital and its links to social capital

Taking a step back, this section defines natural capital in more detail and its fundamental link to social capital. *Natural capital* provides goods and critical 'ecosystem services' essential for a functioning economy,

FIGURE 4. Examples of nature's services.

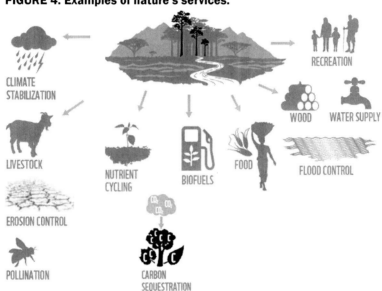

SOURCE: Modified from **Living Planet Report 2014**, p. 89 Figure 54: Ecosystem services ©2014, WWF (panda.org). Some rights reserved.

businesses and society. As illustrated in Figure 4, these include fresh water, productive land for food and fibres, fish, fuels, minerals, sequestration of greenhouse gas (GHG) emissions, clean air, protection against flooding, plants for pharmaceuticals, biodiversity and recreation. These include renewable and non-renewable resources.

Official definitions are below.

> **Natural capital** – the stock of natural assets (air, water, land, habitats) that provide goods and services that benefit society, the economy and business.
>
> **Biodiversity** – the variability among living organisms within and between species and ecosystems. Biodiversity is crucial for healthy ecosystem services.
>
> **Ecosystem services** – the direct and indirect value or benefits people receive from ecosystems. These services are defined as **provisioning**, for example, food and freshwater, **regulating**, for example, climate regulation and flood control and **cultural**, for example, recreation and aesthetic.[25]

Financially valuing natural capital is typically based on the social costs and benefits to effected stakeholders. For example, this could be local communities drawing from the same natural services as the business, for example, a watershed feeding the fresh water supply. Hence, natural capital is fundamentally linked with social capital.

> **Social capital** is the trust across communities and other stakeholder groups businesses interact with. It includes shared values, relationships, reputation, brand and social licence to operate that makes trade, finance, and governance possible.[26]

As illustrated in Figure 5 the environment and its ecosystem services sustain societies that are part of the economy. A key challenge for business

FIGURE 5. Links across Environmental, Social and Economic domains.

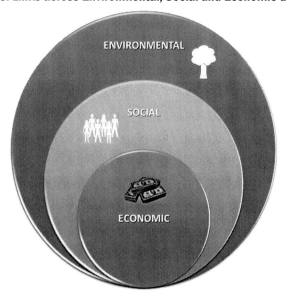

is accounting for capital beyond 'private capital'. This is particularly the case for natural capital as the costs and benefits are to society, as well as the business. Maintaining and enhancing natural capital, where it is lost or degraded, is recognized as essential for sustainable economic growth and the prosperity of business, communities and societies. The problem is that the social costs or benefits of nature's services are externalities not adequately captured in the market.

> **Externalities** – the consequence of an activity that affects parties other than the company undertaking the activity, for which the company is neither compensated nor penalized through the markets. Externalities can be positive, e.g. payments for protecting a watershed, or negative, e.g. health problems for local residents associated with air pollution from a factory.

Scale of the problem

The systems that provide natural capital are degrading and malfunctioning. Looking at the balance of natural capital in planet Earth's bank, we draw down more capital each year than the earth can replenish.[27] More than 60 percent of the vital services provided by nature are in global decline because of overexploitation.[28] Figure 6 illustrates our overshoot per annum of renewable resources and ability to sequester GHG emissions. It shows we are using the equivalent of 1.5 planets that we do not have!

The latest scientific assessment of the Earth's natural systems in *Living Planet Report 2014* (wwf.panda.org/about_our_earth/all_publications/

FIGURE 6. State of the planet from Living Planet Report 2014

OUR DEMAND FOR RENEWABLE ECOLOGICAL RESOURCES AND THE GOODS AND SERVICES THEY PROVIDE IS NOW EQUIVALENT TO MORE THAN 1.5 EARTHS

SINCE THE 1990s WE HAVE REACHED OVERSHOOT BY THE NINTH MONTH EVERY YEAR. WE DEMAND MORE RENEWABLE RESOURCES AND CO₂ SEQUESTRATION THAN THE PLANET CAN PROVIDE IN AN ENTIRE YEAR

SOURCE: Living Planet Report 2014, p. 33 ©2014, WWF (panda.org). Some rights reserved.

living_planet_report/) shows human demand has already exceeded much of the planets ability to replenish. This concludes that:

- Whilst population has risen fourfold in the last century, the water footprint has increased sevenfold;

- Shortages are forecast in 200 of the world's estimated 263 river basins;

- Wildlife populations have more than halved since the 1970s;

- Freshwater species are declining fastest, with three quarters lost since the 1970s.[29]

Evidence studies and business[30] identify urgent natural capital risks including a lack of freshwater, productive land, biodiversity, malfunctioning natural cycles for climate regulation and generation of phosphorous and nitrogen (used in fertilizers for crop production). Four of nine so-called 'planetary boundaries' have been crossed as illustrated in the Stockholm Resilience Centre's Planetary Boundary model[31] in Figure 7.

Business for Social Responsibility (**www.bsr.org/en/collaboration/groups/ecosystem-services-tools-markets**) outline key challenges natural capital malfunction is causing:

The issue today is that too few companies perceive of natural capital risk – or 'ecosystem malfunction risk' (www.economistinsights.com/sustainability-resources/opinion/'laws'-investment) – and its adverse business effects. For example:

- *corporate facilities cooled by ocean water have had to shut down because seawater temperatures have exceed engineering specifications, such as on the coast of the **eastern US** and coast of **France**.[32]*

FIGURE 7. Status of the nine planetary boundaries.

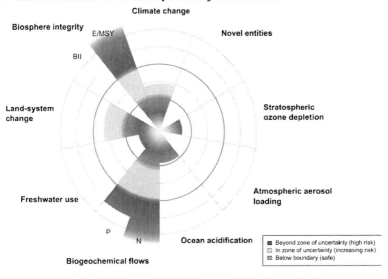

SOURCE: Steffen et al., 16 January 2015, Science, printed with permission.

- *coastal towns, such as in New Jersey during Hurricane Sandy or New Orleans during Hurricane Katrina, which have been catastrophically flooded, with subsequent* **linkages to the dismantling (and dysfunction) of coastal ecosystems and the 'green infrastructure'** *that previously offered coastal areas greater protection and resilience.*[33] ARON CRAMER, PRESIDENT AND CEO, BUSINESS FOR SOCIAL RESPONSIBILITY

In its Global Risks 2015 report,[34] the World Economic Forum identified four of the top 10 risks as sustainability related – water crises, failure of climate change mitigation and adaptation, extreme weather events, biodiversity loss and ecosystem collapse. According to McKinsey's

Resource Revolution, 2013 report (**www.mckinsey.com/insights/energy _resources_materials/resource_revolution_tracking_global_commo dity_markets**), concerns over the future availability of natural resources, for example, food, water, energy and certain minerals, has become particularly acute since 2000 mainly because of rapid growth in demand. Accompanying this have been commodity price increases so significant they eliminate reductions in average commodity prices from the past 100 years![35] In the words of the environmental economist Robert Costanza:

If ecosystem services were actually paid for, in terms of their value contribution to the global economy, the global price system would be very different from what it is today. The price of commodities using ecosystem services directly or indirectly would be much greater. ROBERT COSTANZA ET AL., THE VALUE OF THE WORLD'S ECOSYSTEM SERVICES AND NATURAL CAPITAL, *NATURE*, 1997[36]

PART 2
Sustainability Accounting and Valuation

THIS CHAPTER FOCUSES on the business applications natural and social capital inform and techniques for how to account and value this. As an evolving field, there are many new names emerging for this, for example, 'Triple Bottom Line' (TBL) or Natural Capital Accounting (NCA). Catchy terms for sustainability financial statements are also emerging, such as '**Environmental P&Ls**', '**EP&L**' and '**common good balance sheets**'.[37] Much of what is being called NCA incorporates traditional sustainability and financial accounting approaches with some additional elements included, most notably:

- understanding business dependencies on nature, not just environmental and social impacts, and

- translating this to financial value.

Understanding this can avoid duplication of efforts and facilitate linking company teams across sustainability and finance. Taking this into account, NCA is framed here in the context of 'Sustainability Accounting' which is an integrated approach and familiar to business. It is important to note that methods and metrics are still evolving with many gaps still to fill. Case examples from the following early adopter businesses blazing the trail show the different approaches in use:

- Marks and Spencer

- Otto Group

- Patagonia®

- The Crown Estate

- The Dow Chemical Company

- United Utilities Group.

Business applications

Accounting and valuing natural and social capital informs decision-making in both 'non–financial' and 'financial' terms. This can be used for internal decision-making, management and external communications such as reporting and disclosure. Business use to date focuses mainly on internal applications, rather than external. This is mainly due to a lack of standardized methods and regulatory requirements. Companies start by using natural capital information to inform risk and opportunities in strategic and operational decisions.[38] The different applications natural and social capital can inform are illustrated in Figure 8.

Examples include:

- Strategic hot spot assessments and 'mega trends' planning that informs risks, opportunities and new markets.

- Site, landholding or landscape level decision-making for risk, natural/green infrastructure decisions (such as The Dow Chemical Company), or new market opportunities.

- Supply chain decision-making for risk and procurement (such as apparel companies Kering Group and Otto Group).

- Management accounting – for internal financial decision-making (such as United Utilities Group and The Crown Estate).

- Disclosure externally in sustainability reports and regulated financial accounting/reporting.

- Financial institutions can use natural capital information in ESG assessments for investments or to inform new financial products.

Financial valuation can be reflected in *management accounting* for internal financial decision-making or ultimately for external financial

FIGURE 8. Business applications for natural and social capital inform.

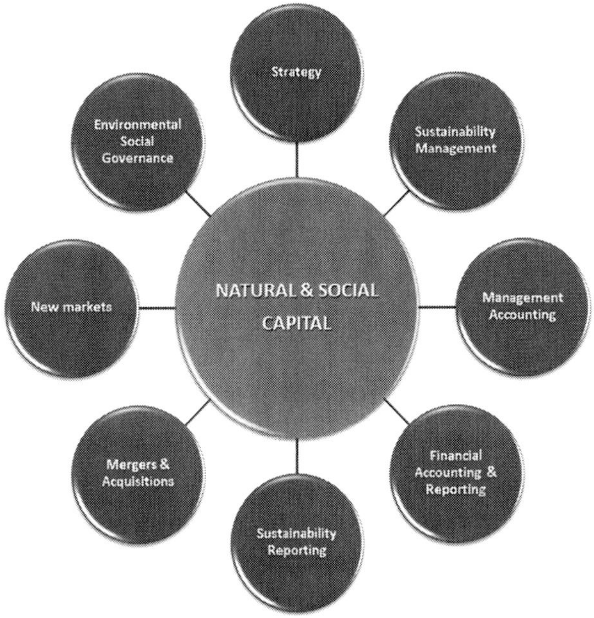

reporting, for example, the balance sheet, profit & loss (P&L) or in the narrative parts of annual reports. The differences between management accounting for internal use and financial accounting for external reporting use are outlined below.

Management accounting – the sourcing, analysis, communication and use of financial and non-financial information to generate and preserve value for organizations.[39] This is used for internal business purposes and is unregulated.

Financial accounting and reporting – the provision of financial information to external stakeholders. It is regulated under two main accounting systems: 1) US Generally **Accepted Accounting Principles (US GAAP)**[40] used in the United States and regulated by the Federal Accounting Standards Body (FASB); and 2) **International Financial Reporting Standards (IFRS)**[41] used in the European Union and many other countries regulated by the International Financial Reporting Standards Body (IASB).[42] Under these, public limited companies are required to produce annual financial accounts including the balance sheet and P&L statement.

Techniques

The aim of sustainability accounting is to understand the environmental, social and economic impacts and dependencies of the business and wider stakeholders impacted – in both non-financial and financial terms. This can inform a range of decisions. Suitable strategies and actions to manage the risks and opportunities assessed can then be taken. Figure 9 illustrates the process.

FIGURE 9. Sustainability accounting informing decision-making – non-financial and financial.

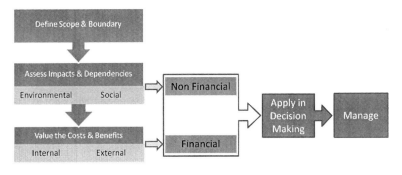

Some of the key techniques used are summarized below to give an overview only. A growing number of guides and tools are available and can be used and examples are given in the Appendix on page 113.

Defining scope and boundary

This involves defining the scope and boundary of the business activities, products and services to be included. This scope can be at the following levels:

- Site specific – at the company factory, site or landholding.

- Landscape level – the scope can include the wider landscape in which the company operates if relevant, such as upstream watersheds if water is drawn from these, or forests, fish stocks, habitats or other impacted ecosystems.

- Supply chain.

The application the information is to be used for will dictate the data and techniques used. For example, the data requirements and reliability needed increase as you move from hot spot assessment to more in-depth applications. Other considerations are the impacted geographic locations, markets, stakeholders and timeline.

Assessing impacts and dependencies

The environmental and social impacts and dependencies should be identified and measured. This provides both qualitative and quantitative non-financial information. Businesses are experienced at assessing their environmental and social *impacts* using indicators based on best practice standards. For environmental impacts, Life Cycle Assessment (LCA), or similar, indicators based on international standards[43] are typically used, for example, Global Warming Potential (GWP) for GHG emissions, waste generation, air and water pollution. For social impacts, standards such as ISO26000 or guides such as Social LCA[44] are used. Recognized tools, standards and data are well developed for this type of impact assessment.

However, environmental management in business normally focuses only on measuring and managing the *impacts* the business has on the external environment. These are an *output* of the business activities. The *outcome* of these environmental impacts on natural, social and other forms of capital is not normally measured. The consequences of changes in the external environment on the business and other stakeholders should be considered. These are the *dependencies* a business has on natural capital and how this effects value creation over time – negatively and positively. The United Utilities Group and The Crown Estate case examples illustrate how they have made this transition to measure and financially value the outcomes of their business activities and include them in management accounting to inform decision-making.

FIGURE 10. Ecosystem Services.

PROVISIONING SERVICES	
Food	crops
	livestock
	capture fisheries
	aquaculture
	wild foods
Fiber	timber
	cotton, silk
	wood fuel
Genetic resources	
Biochemicals, medicines	
Water	freshwater
REGULATING SERVICES	
Air quality regulation	
Climate regulation – global	
Climate regulation –regional and local	
Water regulation	
Erosion regulation	
Water purification and waste treatment	
Disease regulation	
Pest regulation	
Pollination	
Neutral hazard regulation	
CULTURAL SERVICES	
Spiritual and religious values	
Aesthetic values	
Recreation and ecotourism	

SOURCE: Modified from UN Millennium Ecosystem Assessment, 2005 and Common International Classification of Ecosystem Services, 2012.

There are a range of tools and guides for assessing biodiversity and ecosystem services which define indicators to different extents.[45] This is a developing area with many gaps, for example, biodiversity being a particular challenge. Most of these tools have evolved separately from LCA so there is little streamlining of indicators at present. Figure 10 illustrates the ecosystem services categories typically assessed. Only those relevant to the company should be considered. Companies can find assessment of ecosystem services and biodiversity challenging as new questions are being asked. The Patagonia® case illustrates the company's dependence on grassland ecosystem services.

CASE EXAMPLE: Patagonia® *Merino On A Mission*[46] – Maintaining Grassland Ecosystem Services

FIGURE 11.

SOURCE: Photo by Tim Davis, courtesy of Patagonia®.

Outdoor apparel company Patagonia® and partners are regenerating grasslands in Patagonia, southern Argentina. The ecosystem services from these grasslands are essential for continuing to graze successfully the sheep that supply the high-quality merino wool for Patagonia® merino baselayers, sweaters and socks – more than 50 products in all.

Sheep have been grazed in Patagonia since 1888. This has taken a noticeable toll on the semiarid region's fragile grassland. When allowed to graze continually, sheep strip the land of the grass they like best. Without groundcover, rain and wind erode the topsoil, leaving behind bare, unproductive patches of cracked earth. Grasslands sequester carbon, retain moisture, protect the topsoil and provide food and habitat for livestock and wildlife. Besides its value to the planet, grass is essential to the economy of the Patagonia region. Without grass, there would be no natural forage, no jobs for ranch hands, agronomists, wool processors or meatpackers, and no market for all the of goods and services they buy. Patagonia's economy includes oil and gas, mining, fishing, tourism and government jobs, but ranching remains a cornerstone and a way of life.

Since 2010, Patagonia® joined partners Ovis 21 (http://ovis21.com/en/), an Argentine Beneficial Corporation, supporting ranchers on wool, sheep and rangeland management and TNC to regenerate and manage the grasslands. Grasslands scientists from TNC worked with Ovis XXI to review their grazing protocol, known as Holistic Management, and suggested ways to restore trampled creeks and wetlands and bring back some of the pumas and red foxes, guanacos and rheas that have disappeared from loss of habitat and conflicts with ranchers. The result was the Grassland Regeneration and Sustainability Standard known as GRASS (http://ovis21.com/en/alliances). Now, GRASS is producing some of the world's finest merino wool from sheep that are helping to restore the land they graze. By helping to create a market for these merino products, Patagonia® is supporting a regenerative economy that doesn't use the Earth's resources faster than they can be replenished. The goal is to restore 15 million acres of grasslands by 2016.

Valuing costs and benefits

The value of sustainability impacts and dependencies can be measured in non-financial and financial terms. Non-financial are the bio-physical or social metrics determined in the assessment and may be sufficient to inform decision-making without financial valuation.

For financial valuation, there are two main focus areas:

- including *internal* costs and benefits already priced in the market; and

- *externalities* that are not.

- The aim is to calculate the costs and benefits of these to the business and impacted stakeholders. Wider commercial implications, for example, loss of resource supply on operations or reputational damage should also be determined to give a complete financial picture.

There are a growing number of guides and tools for financial valuation (see examples in the Appendix on page 113). The underlying techniques vary and data availability can be a challenge. Some tools only include valuation of environmental impacts and exclude biodiversity and ecosystem services. This is a confusion that business should watch out for.

Internal

Internal costs and benefits are known. The company is aware of and obligated to pay for them because of a market price and/or legal obligation, for example, for carbon emitted, water used or waste management. Costs and benefits can be determined using a range of traditional accounting accounting techniques, such as *Cost–Benefit Analysis (CBA)* and *Environmental Management Accounting (EMA)*.

> **Environmental Management Accounting (EMA)**[47] collects and analyses information for internal decision-making:
>
> i.   physical information on the use, flows and destinies of energy, water and materials (including wastes) and
>
> ii. monetary information on environment-related costs, earnings and savings.
>
> EMA typically involves life-cycle costing, full-cost accounting and benefits assessment.
>
> **Life Cycle Costing** evaluates the costs of an asset throughout its life-cycle – investment, operation, maintenance and end-of-life disposal or recovery.[48,49] Using this approach the cost–benefits of more sustainable options, for example, materials that enable end-of-life recovery for reuse/recycling in a closed loop, can be explicitly included.

Where goods are traded in a market there is an observable market price that reflects the marginal benefit of a good or service. Financial value can be calculated by multiplying the price of the goods/services by the quantity sold and correcting for market distortions, for example, subsidies or taxes. *Net Present Value (NPV)* can be determined, for example, $/ha of harvested timber or minerals. Where the supply is fixed, assigning a value is straightforward. For renewable resources the value of future services can be estimated. Using the accounting practice of *discounting future values*, the current financial value of these benefits can be determined. Market data can be used to identify the value of GHG emissions reduction from carbon pricing or the value of water purification in a wetland using local water pricing.

External

The social costs or benefits of nature's services are externalities not adequately captured in the market. Companies are not obligated to pay these at present and hence they are not typically considered. However, material externalities may ultimately decrease or increase the value of an organization, so assessing their effects in business decision-making is critical. By incorporating natural capital into decision-making, the externalities associated with those decisions can be included, bringing these social costs into the cost–benefit framework. Environmental economic valuation techniques to inform these assessments have been around for many years. However their application in mainstream financial accounting is embryonic. There is ongoing progress to develop innovative ways to capture the value of natural and increasingly social capital, in financial terms. However, formally recognized accounting and valuation methods and policies to establish a *fair value*, or *shadow price* for externalities are all at an early stage.[50] Because most benefits from nature's services are not priced and traded in existing markets, *non-market valuation methods* are used to estimate their value. A summary of these follows.

Valuation methods

Estimating the financial value of nature's services requires an understanding of both bio-physical processes that underpin the provision of those services as well as people's preferences for those services. There are established methods which rely on human preferences either *revealed* (e.g. in market data) or *stated* (e.g. in surveys) to determine value. However, there are many challenges in accurately determining these preferences using these methods.

Revealed preference valuation uses observed spending choices available in *real* or *surrogate* markets to identify their preferences and values. Surrogate markets are used in place of the missing markets for natural capital. *Surrogate market valuation* methods use indirect expenditure data, e.g. the time and money spent to visit a national park indicates how much people value that park. *Hedonic* pricing methods, e.g. how much people are willing to pay for an amenity such as access to a park when choosing a property, can also be used. *Avoided damage costs* or *replacement costs* associated with not having the ecosystem service can be calculated using market and non-market data.

Stated preference methods use surveys to ask people their stated preference values based on hypothetical situations. Consumer surveys are an example. One method is *contingent valuation* which is how much people say they would be *Willing To Pay (WTP)* to preserve something, such as a national park or local green space.

Where there are no data available or fast estimates are needed, the *benefits or values transfer* method is used. This is where existing published estimates of value for an ecosystem service, for example, $/ha of a wetlands, say in Texas, is transferred to another wetland in another location where no valuation has been done. While pragmatic, the downside of benefits transfer is it needs existing reliable valuation data, which are largely not available for ecosystem services. It also does not take into account different geographic conditions which have associated environmental, social and economic implications for determining value. Many of the current tools use benefits transfer to provide a hot spot valuation.

FIGURE 12. Valuation hierarchy (most preferred at the top to least at the bottom).

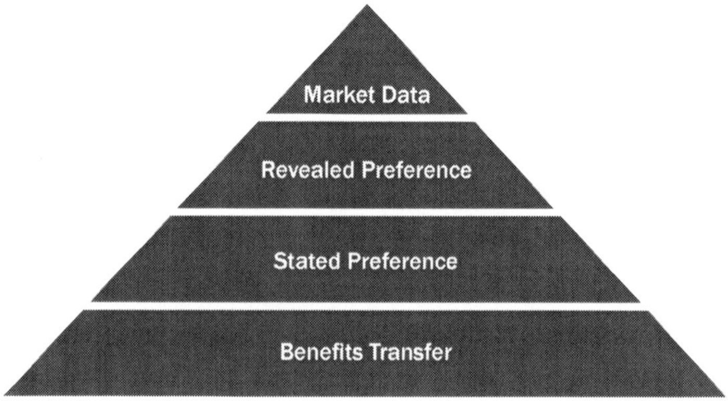

Market Data

Revealed Preference

Stated Preference

Benefits Transfer

The valuation hierarchy normally used is illustrated in Figure 12. The most preferred is market data if available, followed by revealed preference (seen as more reliable than stated preference because of use of actual versus hypothetical market behaviour data). After that, stated preference followed by the least preferred, benefits transfer.

In the United Utilities Group case example, the majority of the values used are based on stated preference data. This originates from their consumer research into customers' WTP for changes in various aspects of water services and levels of environmental quality.

CASE EXAMPLE: United Utilities Triple Bottom Line Accounting

Sustainability accounting today is embryonic – like financial accounting before the Merchants of Venice. In developing Triple Bottom Line accounting we have adopted a principled approach which we hope will contribute to the evolution of global standards. **RUSS HOULDEN, CFO, UNITED UTILITIES GROUP PLC,**

WWW.UNITEDUTILITIES.COM

United Utilities supplies water and wastewater services to a population of around 7 million people in the northwest of England. It uses its assets and technology in combination with the natural environment to become part of the water cycle, collecting water from the environment, purifying it and distributing it to customers and then collecting the wastewater and treating it before returning it to the environment. After treating the wastewater it is left with sludge which it converts to energy for use in its operations, thereby reducing waste and reducing the costs to customers.

FIGURE 13. United Utilities relies on natural capital assets, such as its Haweswater reservoir, to protect and provide great quality water. Haweswater sits in a valley with a fascinating history and is home to some of the UK's rarest and most beautiful wildlife.

SOURCE: Photo permission provided by United Utilities

FIGURE 14. Europe's largest thermal hydrolysis plant at United Utilities' Davyhulme wastewater treatment works, Greater Manchester, England. This award-winning innovative site turns sewage sludge into power.

SOURCE: Photo permission provided by United Utilities

United Utilities has for many years been integrating sustainability thinking into its decision making with tools and techniques such as sustainable cost, sustainable whole-life cost, sustainable NPV, sustainable inputs, sustainable outputs, sustainable catchments and sustainable systems.

Like management accounting, the tools and techniques used for individual decisions are necessarily tailored to the nature of the decision involved. However, for reporting to external stakeholders we recognize the need for global standards of accounting for environmental, social and economic impacts to enable comparability between firms, just as we have global standards for financial accounting. The International Accounting Standards Body (IASB) has not yet extended its remit into this area and the thinking of other bodies in this area is at a very early stage. Indeed, we feel that sustainability accounting today has similarities to financial accounting before the Merchants of Venice.

When we considered this issue in 2012, we saw that the TBL concept had been around for many years but we could not find any firm that had developed the accounting to operationalize the concept. We therefore developed a methodology for TBL accounting which we use internally and which we hope will contribute to the evolution of global standards. Our approach to TBL accounting involves using a principled approach to account for the environmental, social and economic impacts of the firm. Some of the key principles we have adopted are:

1. Boundary – we have accounted for the impact of all entities we control. This mirrors financial accounting.

2. Completeness – we consider all impacts, whether positive or negative, of our business on the environment, society and the economy.

3. Valuation – we measure impacts based on outcomes, not outputs, and we measure the value of outcomes in monetary

terms based entirely on fair value, using a preference hierarchy of valuation techniques, which is analogous to the valuation hierarchies used in financial accounting.

4. Materiality – we have only accounted for impacts which are material in the context of our total impact. Unlike all retailers and most manufacturers, the impacts of our business upstream and downstream in the water cycle are much larger than the impacts of our supply chain.

5. Time period – in view of the very long-term nature of the decisions we take, with typical asset lives of 20–100 years and impacts over a similar timeframe, we felt that the accounting year in financial accounting was too short for us and we therefore adopted a five year time period reflecting the regulatory asset management periods in our industry.

6. Confidence – in order to ensure that we and all stakeholders would have confidence in our valuations, we used leading academic, economic and environmental experts to validate and assure our approach.

With TBL accounting we have been able to estimate the impact of the sum of all of the decisions we have taken and will take in the 2010–2020 period in terms of total value added (environmental, societal and economic). This has been a helpful test that the sum of thousands of individual decisions is resulting in real benefits for the environment, for society and for the economy.

CASE EXAMPLE: Dow Chemical Company

Dow believes that valuing nature makes good business sense. Valuing natural capital and ecosystem services helps Dow make better business decisions for Dow, for our communities, and for the planet we share.
MARK WEICK, DIRECTOR, SUSTAINABILITY PRO-GRAMS AND ENTERPRISE RISK MANAGEMENT, THE DOW CHEMICAL COMPANY, *WWW.DOW.COM*

The Dow Chemical Company (Dow) is actively developing an approach to value ecosystem services and incorporate these valuations in business decisions. As part of this strategic emphasis, a financial and environmental analysis of the use of a constructed wetland for industrial wastewater treatment at their Seadrift, Texas manufacturing site was conducted in 2013.

In 1996, Dow's Seadrift site needed to improve the level of tertiary water treatment to meet EPA effluent guidelines for suspended solids consisting mostly of algae in approximately 5 million gallons a day of industrial wastewater. The site had essentially two choices to solve the problem. The typical industrial Wastewater Treatment Plant designed to remove organic material and eliminate flows through the ponds that create algae naturally had a capital cost estimate of approximately $40 MM. This option would also involve operational and maintenance costs that were estimated to be higher than the second option – converting 110 acres of an existing treatment pond into constructed wetlands at a capital cost of about $1.4 MM.

The 2013 study used Replacement Cost Methodology (RCM) for financial analysis and Life Cycle Assessment (LCA) for environmental assessment. The financial results indicate that the total NPV savings calculated for implementing the constructed wetland instead of the sequencing batch reactor is $282 million over the project's lifetime. The LCA demonstrates that the lower energy and material inputs to the constructed wetland resulted in lower potential impacts for fossil fuel use, acidification, smog formation and ozone depletion and likely lead to lower potential impacts for global warming and marine eutrophication. The result from the inventory of land use shows that both the upstream land burdens (for the sequencing batch reactor) and the on-site acreage of the constructed wetland are similar in magnitude and importance, contrary to the assumption that green infrastructure always requires greater land

FIGURE 15. Constructed wetlands option versus effluent treatment plant.

VS

SOURCE: Photos provided with permission from Dow Chemical Company

area. The area serves as great habitat for fish, alligators, raccoons, bobcats, deer and a large number of birds. More detail on the case has been published in the *Journal of Industrial Ecology*.[51]

CASE EXAMPLE: Making a Positive Impact – The Crown Estate's Total Contribution

For me sustainability is a central driving factor behind our strategy and our long-term commercial success. Total Contribution has helped us to take a more rounded look at how we measure the value this creates – going beyond just the numbers and fulfilling the old adage, we treasure what we measure.

ALISON NIMMO, CEO, THE CROWN ESTATE, *WWW.THECROWNESTATE.CO.UK*

The Crown Estate is an independent commercial business in the UK created by an Act of Parliament (1961). Its business includes the whole of London's Regent Street, much of St James, Glenlivet, Windsor Great Park, numerous regional shopping centres, hundreds of thousands of acres of rural land and coastline, and the UK's seabed. Its role is to make sure that the land and property it invests in and manages are sustainably worked, developed and enjoyed to deliver the best value over the long term.

The Crown Estate's revenue profit is paid to the UK Treasury for the benefit of the public finances, but like many other companies its activities contribute significantly more than just financial return. In order to measure this broader value as well as influence and improve decision-making and performance it has developed an approach called *Total Contribution*.

This considers the business's economic, environmental and social impacts and dependencies. It covers the full value chain: from direct operations through to the indirect activities of the supply chain and the 'enabled activities' of others on The Crown Estate's land. It is based upon a framework of principles:

- **Credit** – clearly setting out and defining the boundaries of the scope, including what the business is accountable for and where it has control or influence. Telling the full story, but not aggregating the results.

- **Confidence** – how confident the business is in the results, particularly identifying where it is relying on modelling and assumptions.

- **Net contribution** – taking into account the negative as well as positive outcomes of the business's activities, including connected activity elsewhere and things that 'would have happened anyway'.

A 26-strong team came together to develop the approach. They were supported by external consultants, NEF consulting, and their partners Route2Sustainability and Landman Economics. The first step was to identify the activities that The Crown Estate undertakes that are most relevant to the business. Much of this was already being collected but it also provided a good review of information requirements.

Once the indicators were identified the next step was to think about how to move these from measuring not just what occurs (output), but the value or outcome from an activity. For example, rather than measuring the amount of people visiting a location because of the natural beauty, the 'outcome' would be the value derived by attendees from their experience. Another example would be taking a strong Corporate Responsibility story, such as the 730 people The Crown Estate has helped to find work on Regent Street, and identifying that this equates to a £6.8 million contribution to the UK economy. The value can be qualitative, quantitative, or a monetary valuation. The Crown Estate used acknowledged existing models to do this and clearly published the models and any assumptions made. The indicators used are below.

	Economic Indicators	Gross Value Added Employment Investment Contribution to Her Majesty's Treasury
	Environmental Indicators	Electricity Generated Greenhouse gas emissions CO_2 sequestered Greenhouse emissions avoided Water consumption Waste Biodiversity
	Social Indicators	Gross Value Added Educational Visitors Destination Visitors Community Benefits

This has been a real cross-business initiative, with each function bringing specific skills to the table. Whilst the sustainability team came up with the ideas and highlighted the broader value, the Finance team brought the rigour, systems and process to enable this to become part of how we do business.

JOHN LELLIOTT, FINANCE DIRECTOR, THE CROWN ESTATE

Total Contribution has provided many benefits: including allowing broader implications to be taken into account during business planning, thereby improving business resilience and building

FIGURE 16. Windsor Great Park.

SOURCE: Printed with permission of The Crown Estate

stronger relationships with our partners. Employees are now offered participatory training so that they can work more closely with partners in the value chain and the Total Contribution is considered when putting together any new business case.

The measurement of The Crown Estate's significant natural resources has been an important element of Total Contribution. It has prompted a review of risks and opportunities and the development of innovative leases that reward tenants for improvements in natural capital. This in turn preserves the long-term financial value of the business's assets. A pilot study has been carried out on the Windsor Estate, part of the rural portfolio, to identify the high environmental and cultural value not fully reflected in the financial accounts at present. A top-down approach was taken using detailed GIS mapping and an external ecosystem service valuation model (UK National Ecosystem Assessment[52]). This was due to the resource considerations of applying it across the whole portfolio which would involve numerous sites. It identified:

- The enjoyment of about 3 million visits to Windsor Great Park annually, valued at an additional £1.9 million per year.

- The role of trees in filtering local air pollution and avoiding health impacts from respiratory diseases, valued at £0.4 million per year.

- The enjoyment of people in the surrounding area from the view of the Park, valued at £0.6 million per year.

- The soils and vegetation on site store and sequester carbon, contributing to a reduction in greenhouse gases and resulting climate change valued at £2.3/ha/year on average.

Taking account of these wider social values, the Windsor Estate delivers a significant net benefit to society. This is equal to £4.4 million per annum gross external benefit and when delivered as a corporate natural capital account the asset value is £45.6 million (present value terms) over 100 years. The reporting statements record the net benefits that accrue to The Crown Estate and the external values that the Park delivers to the local community, visitors, and globally.

Many of the concepts included in Total Contribution were not new. It gained traction because it was communicated in a simple and transparent way that everyone could understand. MARK GOUGH, HEAD OF SUSTAINABILITY, THE CROWN ESTATE

CASE EXAMPLE: Sustainability at the Otto Group – A matter of measure and management

Measuring environmental and social impacts combined with stakeholder assessments allows us now to treat and address sustainability as a conventional management issue. Furthermore, by assessing our environmental impact through monetary terms we are also able to communicate our insights much better internally. DR JOHANNES MERCK, VICE PRESIDENT SUSTAINABILITY, OTTO GROUP, *WWW.OTTOGROUP.COM*

Otto Group at a glance

With 12 billion Euros revenue in 2013/14, the family-owned Otto Group is one of the biggest e-commerce companies worldwide. It has activities in more than 20 countries and listed companies, such as OTTO, bonprix, Hermes and Crate & Barrel in the three core segments – multichannel retail, financial services and services. The group employs more than 53,000 people and has over 50 million customers a year. At Otto Group, sustainability is a priority from the top for many years with Dr Michael Otto (chairman of the supervisory board), a sustainability pioneer in his own right. In 2014 the Otto Group received the CSR award of the German Federal Government for 'impACT', the CR-management-process, including an innovative approach of assessing the social and environmental impact of the entire Otto Group.

Switching from traditional sustainability management to the innovative impACT-process

The Otto Group's sustainability management traditionally focused on two approaches – stakeholder dialogue and technical impact assessment, such as LCA. Even though both are well developed, experience shows that results and their ability to inform management decision making can be improved. Against this background the Otto Group introduced 'estell' (**www.systain.com/en/applied-methodologies/estell/**) developed by Systain consultancy. This assesses environmental and social impacts and prioritizes material actions for management. Key features are that it covers the group's entire value chain including the supply chain (upstream) and the use phase of products (downstream). Environmental impacts are quantified on the basis of 'external costs', a concept that accounts for the fact that business activities impose a cost upon a third party not covered in the direct operational costs. Social risks (impacts) are quantified based on 'risk hours', where products or services originate under specifically risky working conditions (e.g. low wage, physically harmful, etc.). The advantage of estell's approach is that it can be efficiently applied in complex company structures and enables better internal communication based on both monetary valuation and impacts data. Drawing from financial company data, usually available in the financial accounting department, estell relates these data to global economic activities based on a multi-regional input output model. The results are presented in a *Sustainability Impact Scorecard*. Externalities are classified and arranged according to their environmental or social nature as well as their location in the value chain.

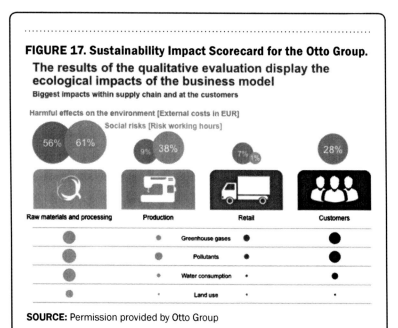

FIGURE 17. Sustainability Impact Scorecard for the Otto Group. The results of the qualitative evaluation display the ecological impacts of the business model

Biggest impacts within supply chain and at the customers

SOURCE: Permission provided by Otto Group

With impACT the Otto Group has reset its sustainability management using the following:

- **Materiality and strategic positioning** – On the basis of the results of the Sustainability Impact Scorecard, a Materiality Matrix (Figure 18) is used to identify material issues quantitatively and qualitatively. The quantitative is based on external costs for environment, and risk working hours for social issues. The qualitative on continuous stakeholder dialogue and internal reviews focusing on reputational and regulatory issues. Each issue is categorised as: priority, innovation, base and stop.

FIGURE 18. Materiality Matrix by the Otto Group (sample evaluation).

The results of the quantitative and qualitative evaluation lead to the Materiality Matrix of the Otto Group

Sample evaluation and strategic classification of external impacts

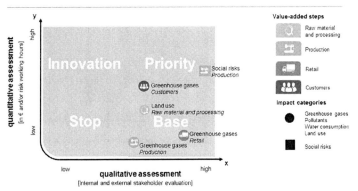

SOURCE: Permission provided by Otto Group

- **Development and assessment of measures** – Current and potential measures are assessed to reduce sustainability impacts using LCA or estell to determine external cost figures or risk hours.

- **Implementation under the framework of a single sustainability strategy** – Material issues are addressed by the most efficient measures and related to specific targets. Performance monitoring and reporting show progress.

The Otto Group case shows how the company assesses environmental and social issues and costs across the supply chain – internal and externalities. This has informed assessment and prioritization of material issues with the common language of money facilitating internal communications.

CASE EXAMPLE: Marks and Spencer Net Benefit Approach

Sustainability is both a moral and commercial imperative – in short, there is a business case for going green. ADAM ELMAN, GLOBAL HEAD OF DELIVERY – PLAN A, MARKS & SPENCER PLC, *HTTP://CORPORATE.MARKSANDSPENCER.COM/ PLAN-A*

Marks and Spencer – Plan A

Marks and Spencer (M&S) is an international multi-channel retailer of stylish, high quality, great value clothing, home products and outstanding quality food, responsibly sourced from around 3,000 suppliers globally. Plan A was launched in January 2007, making 100 social and environmental commitments to be delivered by March 2012. It's called Plan A because there is no Plan B when it comes to conserving the Earth's finite resources. It has recently been updated (now Plan A 2020) to ensure the companies goals are reflective of new challenges and opportunities.

Business case for going green

There is a perception (an incorrect one!) that going green costs more and therefore balance sheet pressures dictate going with the status quo of doing business. M&S's view couldn't be more different – sustainability is both a moral and commercial imperative. *In short, there is a business case for going green.* In the short term, it is about insulating your business from cost pressures; in the longer term, a more sophisticated business case has emerged, predicated on opportunity, innovation and new revenue streams.

Managing the process and engaging finance

A lesson learnt early on with Plan A, is that it needed to be managed as a cross-business change programme. To be successful, it could not be a CSR initiative that resided with a small team on the side of the business. As such, all of the standard governance, process and tracking tools that any business would use when undertaking a large change programme of this type were used.

At the launch of Plan A, £200 million (£40 million a year over the initial five years) was set aside. With 100 work streams across the business, there was a significant risk that costs would run out of control without this discipline. Careful tracking of who was spending it and on what was a necessity. Given that Plan A cuts across every part of the business, the Finance Department were engaged with to help with this tracking. They had the knowledge, skills and experience needed as well as embedded analytics right across the business.

Measuring true costs and benefits

At the start of the process, developing a 'business case' was not the intent, but it made sense to start asking what benefit was also being delivered. This was not as easy as it sounds, as a methodology had to be developed for capturing the true costs and benefits. This covered activities as diverse as energy reduction to food life extension and recycling, each requiring its own calculation and baseline. Techniques such as whole life costing were used in conjunction with robust non-financial data including LCA. M&S specifically focused on absolute costs rather than estimating externalities.

FIGURE 19. M&S Sustainable Store Cheshire Oaks.

SOURCE: Printed with permission from Marks and Spencer Plc

In only its second year, it became clear that Plan A was delivering significant cost–benefits. To add to that it was opening up new revenue streams that were taking off. In year three it returned a net benefit to the business, or profit if you like, and has delivered one every year since. Last year (2013/14) the net benefit was £145 million and over the seven years in total, the benefit is £465 million ($US701 million). That's £465 million that M&S would either have had to find from elsewhere or simply would not have had in the first place. The savings made include being more energy efficient, using less fuel, recycling and reusing clothes hangers, reducing waste, using less packaging and more. But it's not just financial savings; M&S saw many other benefits such as increased staff motivation, brand enhancement and supply chain resiliency to name a few.

Business case for suppliers

M&S suppliers – many of them small businesses – are also involved in Plan A and are making their businesses more efficient and more profitable. One example is West Mill, a hosiery factory in Belper, Derbyshire, which was on the brink of closure a few years ago. Now it has turned its fortunes around by controlling its energy use, slashing £2 million from its annual bills. It was awarded eco-factory status by M&S meaning that every product produced at the factory can be labelled as having a Plan A attribute – boosting the marketing power of the factory's products.

Next steps

Going forward, as a consequence of interconnected opportunities and risks, business models will be disrupted by sustainability for the first time. Monetizing the long-term business benefit is a challenge, but irrespective, our use of the word 'disruption' highlights just how crucial the business case for sustainability will become in the future. At M&S, the core purpose of business is to enhance lives every day and by doing this we will prosper. The next stage of our plan – Plan A 2020, aims to help accelerate our sustainability efforts. It's organized around four pillars, Inspiration, In Touch, Integrity and Innovation, and supports our aspiration to become the world's most sustainable major retailer.

PART 3

Drivers and Current Context

THIS CHAPTER PROVIDES AN OVERVIEW on the current context framing natural capital and key emerging drivers business should watch. Key topics are:

- Natural capital state of play.

- Drivers from policy, market incentives and pressure for greater transparency and accountability.

- Bigger picture shift to business models for value creation.

State of play

Irrespective of the fact that the natural capital concept has existed for many years, its application in policy and business is only starting to gain traction and at an early stage of development. Social capital applications in business are at an even earlier stage. As illustrated in Figure 19, from a business perspective, the current context is like a jigsaw with many fragmented initiatives and limited incentives for action. However, drivers are growing from Green Economy/'Beyond GDP' policy, market incentives and pressure for greater accountability through reporting and disclosure.

FIGURE 20. Natural capital initiatives and incentives.

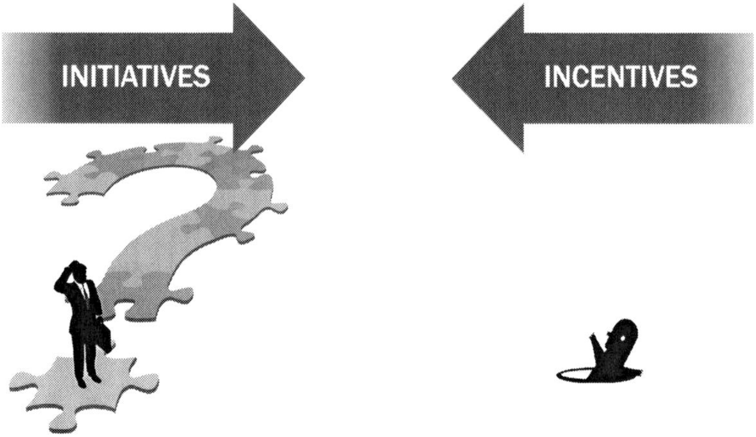

SOURCE: Image from Dreamstime used under standard Content Usage Agreement

There are a confusing array of initiatives, guides and tools from NGOs, government, research and consultancies focusing on different business, finance and policy applications of natural capital accounting and valuation – over 100 at last count![53],[54] For many years government, NGOs and academia have been researching the science, developing the evidence base and tools to support measurement, management and valuation of ecosystem services and biodiversity. Examples include World Resource Institute (**www.wri.org/tags/ecosystem-services**), WBCSD Corporate Ecosystem Valuation and Redefining Value (**www.wbcsd. org/financialcapital.aspx**), UNEP TEEB (The Economics of Ecosystems and Biodiversity),[55] Natural Capital Project (**www.naturalcapitalproject. org**), and IUCN (**www.iucn.org/about/work/programmes/ecosystem_ management/**). Guidance on techniques to monetize environmental impacts, such as Life Cycle Costing has come from environmental economics and LCA practitioners. Overall, interest from mainstream business has been limited, but this is changing as natural capital moves up the business agenda.[56] Business initiatives for awareness raising and development of metrics are growing and increasingly focus on CFOs and financial functions, as well as sustainability, such as Natural Capital Coalition (**www.naturalcapitalcoalition.org**), Accounting for Sustainability CFO's Leadership Network (**www.accountingforsustainability.org**) and Natural Capital Declaration (includes 41 financial institutions; **www.naturalcapitaldeclaration.org**). The corporate reporting, finance and accounting communities play an increasingly prominent role in this area. International representation across many of these business initiatives is growing with activity in Europe, USA and South America. Most of these engage corporations across multiple sectors. However, a few sector specific initiatives are in place for the finance, energy, mining and fisheries sectors in particular. Links to further resources are in the Appendix on page 113.

Despite this activity, natural capital is still largely new to target user communities in business and finance. Complex terminology and silos of activity mean there is a lack of clarity in business on the fundamentals of what natural and social capital are, where they fit in the existing sustainability and financial toolbox and how to use them to inform better decisions. There is also ongoing debate on the ethics of monetary valuation of nature and whether it can really drive sustainability improvements in practice.

There are no recognized standards for natural capital accounting and valuation methods yet, but several initiatives are focusing on this at present. Some to watch are:

- The EU Business and Biodiversity Platform's Natural Capital Accounting draft guidance and tool for selecting approaches.[57]

- The UK Natural Capital Committee guidelines for Developing Corporate Natural Capital Accounts[58] for corporations and large landowners to account for natural capital assets and liabilities in a balance sheet format.

- The Natural Capital Coalition's (**www.naturalcapitalcoalition.org**) Natural Capital Protocol framework for Natural Capital Accounting is underway and expected in 2016.

- Natural Capital Declaration (**www.naturalcapitaldeclaration.org**) ongoing work to develop standard methods for integrating natural capital in financial institutions.

Views on the state of play in business from key initiatives are described.

A growing number of CFOs and Boards recognise the business case for valuing natural and social capital to gain new insight into business risk and opportunity – in particular within sectors with a heavy reliance on nature and where trust has been damaged. As A4S research has shown, many more remain to be convinced. Finance professionals struggle with the multiplicity of accounting and reporting frameworks, the lack of consistent approaches, and the 'insider' terminology frequently used. More than anything, they just aren't being asked to provide support. JESSICA FRIES, EXECUTIVE CHAIRMAN, THE PRINCE'S ACCOUNTING FOR SUSTAINABILITY PROJECT

Today too few companies perceive of natural capital risk and its adverse business effects. Awareness of these facts is growing

fast. More and more, CEOs and Boards are looking for tools to measure and place a value on natural capital, so that they can use this as a crucial element of investment decisions. As the concept of natural capital valuation takes hold, companies can assess risks more accurately, and do what they are best at – look for the new opportunities. ARON CRAMER, PRESIDENT AND CEO, BUSINESS FOR SOCIAL RESPONSIBILITY

Businesses are becoming increasingly sensitized to the risks associated with depending on the natural world for products and services. Thinking about nature as a capital asset – something which is properly valued and protected – helps a business become more resilient and profitable in the long run. STUART POORE, DIRECTOR OF CORPORATE SUSTAINABILITY, WWF-UK

Green Economy & beyond GDP/GNP

Current Green Economy and Green Growth policies aim to address a variety of market, policy and institutional failures that drive natural capital degradation without paying the true social costs of depletion, and without adequate reinvestment in other forms of wealth. These include many measures from a range of stakeholders, for example, ending government subsidies that promote wasteful use of fuel and other resources, more investment in green technologies and infrastructure. According to the Green Economy Coalition (**www.greeneconomycoalition.org**):

Natural systems support all societies and economies. To understand this dependency and to quantify what investment is needed by whom to ensure continued provision of natural

system services is the most fundamental component of a green economy. In short, we need to sort out, urgently, how to measure natural capital, how to report it, trade in it, protect it and make all of this relevant to people, companies, investors and legislators.

OLIVER GREENFIELD, CONVENOR, GREEN ECONOMY COALITION

As part of government activities to drive these policies, accounting mechanisms to value natural assets and 'Beyond GDP/GNP' or 'GDP Plus' indicators of performance, are being put in place in over 20 countries to date. This includes the EU, Canada, Mexico, Colombia, the Philippines, and South Africa. In the UK for example, a National Ecosystem Assessment (**http://uknea.unep-wcmc.org/About/tabid/56/Default. aspx**) approach, Ecosystems Market Task Force (**https://www.gov.uk/ government/groups/ecosystem-markets-task-force#role-of-the-group**) and Natural Capital Committee (**https://www.naturalcapitalcommittee. org**) support government to integrate natural capital into UK national accounts and market activities. Key elements of policy activity are the roll out of the System of Environmental and Economic Accounts (SEEA),[59] the linked World Bank Wealth Accounting and Valuation of Ecosystem Services (WAVES)[60] global programme and the Convention on Biological Diversity (CBD; **www.cbd.int/ecosystem/**). These focus on ensuring valuation of natures assets are reflected in national growth strategies and accounts. Overall, this will support the development of policy, natural asset pricing and indicators to track progress on reversing natural capital degradation. The ability of this to enable resource targets and taxation for business is a potential driver to watch for the future. As noted by Nobel Laureate economist Joseph Stiglitz, moving 'Beyond GDP' will give a much more informed view of national assets:

A private company is judged by both its income and balance sheet, but most countries only compile an income statement (GDP) and know very little about the national balance sheet.
JOSEPH STIGLITZ, *WWW.JOSEPHSTIGLITZ.COM*

Market incentives

Voluntary markets to incentivize GHG emissions reduction, protect water quality, biodiversity[61] and forest conservation, for example, UN REDD (Reducing Emissions from Deforestation and forest Degradation)[62] are growing internationally.[63] Mandatory schemes for regulating GHG emissions exist in some countries, such as the EU Emissions Trading Scheme (EU ETS). Overall, through these schemes payments or credits, which can be traded or offset, are designed to create a market incentive to protect versus damage nature, however results so far are mixed. Taking carbon as an example, the general view is that the carbon price is an under valuation and too variable. This, along with the lack of a global mandatory scheme and carbon market, is a reason for carbon pricing having a limited impact in incentivizing GHG emissions reductions worldwide. Green investment opportunities are another growing incentive to protect natural capital and finance conservation. One example is the Latin American Water Funds Partnership[64] led by consumer company FEMSA which has leveraged US$27 million in regional water funds to protect watersheds in Brazil.

Payments for Ecosystem Services (PES) schemes for water quality protection and forest conservation, present a growing opportunity with 300 estimated to operate around the world.[65] They involve payments to the managers of land or other natural resources in exchange for the provision of specified services, such as water quality regulation or provision of habitat for wildlife. This means that those who provide ecosystem services are paid for doing so. Payments are made by the beneficiaries of the services in question, for example, individuals, communities, businesses or governments acting on behalf of various parties. This is the 'beneficiary pays principle' as distinct from the more traditional 'polluter pays principle' used for environmental protection to date. PES provides an opportunity to put a price on previously un-priced ecosystem services and brings them into the wider economy. Figure 21 illustrates the PES concept for watershed services.

FIGURE 21. PES Concept for Watershed services.

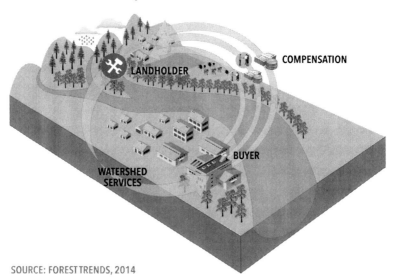

SOURCE: FOREST TRENDS, 2014

SOURCE: Gaining Depth: State of Watershed Investment 2014[66]
© Ecosystem Marketplace, printed with permission

Business PES water examples include Vitell in France and South West Water in the UK. The Brazilian Business and Ecosystem Services Partnership – Parceria Empresarial Pelos Serviços Ecossistêmicos (PESE; **www. wri.org/our-work/project/brazilian-business-and-ecosystem-services-partnership**) including Wal-Mart Brazil, Anglo American, Danone and Andre Maggi Group is focusing on avoiding deforestation in the Amazon.

> *Payments for Ecosystem Services – A paradigm shift from the traditional 'polluter pays principle' to the 'beneficiary pays principle'.*

Transparency and accountability

The accounting, finance and reporting communities are strong advocates of natural capital accounting and valuation for reporting and disclosure purposes – both non-financial and financial. This is in the interests of transparency and accountability as part of wider CSR strategies. For investors, in particular, it provides a mechanism for identifying and rewarding socially responsible business that can drive sustainable investment. IDB describe how investing in natural capital can drive sustainable business:

We are building up a track record that shows to the private sector that investing in natural capital is profitable. Through energy use, we've successfully demonstrated that investing in energy efficiency and renewable energy is good for the climate and for our clients. Financing rooftop solar or a new biodigester is becoming core to smarter, more sustainable business. We need to make that same case with natural capital. HANS SCHULZ, VICE PRESIDENT FOR THE PRIVATE SECTOR AND NON-SOVEREIGN GUARANTEED OPERATIONS, IDB

The accounting profession see a growing role for integration of natural capital in management accounting for internal financial decision-making. If financial accounting and reporting regulatory bodies mandate it and put in place recognized standards, use in financial accounting and reporting is expected to grow. Accounting profession institutes describe the rationale for natural capital integration in accounting and reporting and the key role accountants play.

> *Biodiversity and ecosystem externalities should be fully inte-grated and accounted for in risk and materiality assessments and subsequent reporting cycles. Professional accountants in business are well placed to apply their core skills and expertise to quantify and manage such externalities in order to internalize impacts on biodiversity and ecosystem services.* RACHEL JACKSON, HEAD OF SUSTAINABILITY, ACCA
>
> *The true cost to society from the impact of business activity on natural resources is not reflected in corporate accounts. Accountants, especially those in leadership roles, have a vital role in helping their organizations navigate through the risks and opportunities that natural capital depletion will create. Accountants must incorporate natural resource considerations into strategic planning, business decisions and reporting. They have the skills and oversight to robustly make the connections between natural capital, commercial opportunity and risk, and ultimately financial performance.* SANDRA RAPACIOLI, HEAD OF SUSTAINABILITY RESEARCH AND POLICY, CIMA

> *To ensure their organizations are more resilient, managers need to take into account natural capital in decision-making and the reporting narrative. Natural capital remains largely absent from public disclosures to investors and other stakeholders. Driven by conventional accounting and regulation, an organization's external reporting typically focuses on accounting for private capital owned by the organization and its investors. Over the last 15 or so years, this has started to change with an increasing number of organizations providing information on their environmental, social, and economic impacts in separate corporate responsibility, accountability, or sustainability reports, and more recently in integrated reports. Being transparent is an opportunity to show how an organization is innovating and adapting.* STATHIS GOULD, HEAD OF PAIB, INTERNATIONAL FEDERATION OF ACCOUNTANTS

Mandatory reporting of non-financial information including environmental and social criteria is in place on a 'report or explain basis' in several countries including China, South Africa and Denmark.[67] Singapore is one of the most recent to follow suit. The Singapore Stock Exchange CEO notes the rationale as:

> *Investors are more likely to sell companies that are not green, so while sustainability reporting is an opportunity for green companies to showcase their effort on a global stage, it is also a threat to companies that are not sustainable.* MAGNUS BOCKER, CEO, SINGAPORE EXCHANGE (SGX) FROM SGX TO MAKE SUSTAINABILITY REPORTING MANDATORY, 2014[68]

In the EU, the 2014 Directive on non-financial information reporting[69] makes it mandatory for public companies with over 300 employees to report annually on policies, outcomes and risks associated with environmental, social and wider governance issues. This is an important milestone for driving mandatory reporting. To support this, many business focused guides, tools and schemes are in place for voluntary non-financial reporting and disclosure of sustainability, such as Integrated Reporting (IR; www.iirc.org) Framework, Global Reporting Initiative (GRI; https://www.globalreporting.org) guidelines and standards/guides for specific impacts, for example, CDP (https://www.cdp.net). Inclusion of natural capital is an increasing focus of these. For example, the Climate Disclosure Standards Board (CDSB) Framework (www.cdsb.net/cdsb-reporting-framework) method for disclosure incorporates natural capital and wider environmental information in an organization's mainstream report. Mardi O'Brien, MD, CDSB describes the key elements required:

> *To equate natural capital with financial capital, as equally and collectively essential for an understanding of corporate and sustainability performance, organizations must report on their impacts and dependencies. Standardized disclosure is needed, which can complement and supplement other information in mainstream reports by including information on: organizational boundaries, materiality, governance, policy, strategy, risks, opportunities and performance.* MARDI MCBRIEN, MANAGING DIRECTOR, CLIMATE DISCLOSURE STANDARDS BOARD

For investors ESG risk assessment frameworks, ratings schemes and Socially Responsible Investment (SRI) activities are growing but translation of natural and social capital considerations into the financial terms investors use are at an early stage. Framework principles to assess environmental and social risk in non-financial terms are in place, for example, the Equator Principles (**www.equator-principles.com**) and UN Principles for Responsible Investment (UNPRI; **www.unpri.org**) supported by more detailed guidance, such as the IFC Performance Standard 6[70] that incorporates ecosystem services and biodiversity. Initiatives such as the Sustainable Accounting Standards Board (SASB; **www.sasb.org**) Materiality Maps™[71] aim to clarify the relative priority of sustainability issues across industries and sectors. At a broader financial sector level initiatives such as the Sustainable Stock Exchange (**www.sseinitiative. org**) bring investors, regulators, and companies together to focus on enhancing corporate transparency, ESG performance and responsible long-term approaches to investment. Sixteen exchanges including London (LSE) and the NASDAQ OMX are participating to date. Outside of guidance and schemes, the growing announcements on divestment from fossil fuels related investments, for example, from the Rockefeller Foundation and several universities is making investors stand up and take notice. In particular the September 2014 Global Investors Statement on Climate Change[72] from over 300 global institutional investors representing over $24 trillion in assets asking for carbon pricing inclusion in investment decisions is an important milestone. In the statement these investors commit the inclusion of costs of climate change risks in investment decisions and asking governments in upcoming climate treaty negotiations for global carbon pricing. Their rationale is that stable, reliable and economically meaningful carbon pricing will help them redirect investment commensurate with the scale of the climate change challenge.

Emerging business models for value creation

At the bigger picture, an increasing driver is the shift in business models to focus on 'value creation'. This is evolving with natural and social capital as a core element. Key developments include:

- Integrated business models linking the *six capitals* of business to support *Integrated Thinking* and *Integrated Reporting*.

- The use of integrated metrics, non-financial and financial, to support effective decision-making.

- Doing less bad and more good – shifting away from environmental impact reduction to creating a 'Net Positive' or 'Net Benefit' for nature.

- Shifting from short- to long-term investment cycles, and linking remuneration/bonuses to non-financial or long-term performance indicators.

- Rebooting the purpose of economies, capital markets and business within frameworks that deliver societal well-being, healthy ecosystems, resilience, employment, equality and prosperity, now and in the future.

Integration of capitals and metrics

Integrating natural and social capital in business models is part of a wider shift to business models where the interactions across the six capitals of business (financial, manufactured, human, intellectual, social and natural) are considered. This 'integrated thinking' underpins the *Integrated Reporting <IR>* framework which a growing number of businesses are piloting internationally.[73] As illustrated in Figure 22 in this business model, the capitals are *inputs* used by business, not only to create outputs, but *value* across these capitals over time.

FIGURE 22. The Value Creation Process in the <IR> Framework.

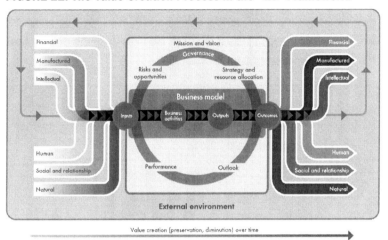

SOURCE: Copyright © December 2013 by the International Integrated Reporting Council ('the IIRC'). All rights reserved. Used with permission of the IIRC.

Leading businesses understand the drivers of value – all the capitals they use and affect – and the impact, including risks, they have on their business model. These in turn are leading to strategic benefits, including better decision-making, under-standing of risks and opportunities and better engagement with the board about goals and targets. PAUL DRUCKMAN, CEO, INTERNATIONAL INTEGRATED REPORTING COUNCIL

Doing more good and less bad

In terms of the value creation of a business and sustainability manage-ment, the trend is to move away from the 'doing less bad' approach of impact reduction to 'enhancing' the environment and society with which a business interacts. Approaches such as DIY retailer Kingfisher Group's 'Net Positive', Marks and Spencer's 'Net Benefit', Rio Tinto's commitment to having a 'Net Positive Impact (NPI)' on biodiversity or the 'No Net Loss (NNL)' of biodiversity concept are examples.

> The Kingfisher Group aim is to be Net Positive across its businesses including timber, where it aims to create more forests than it uses and only use certified sustainable sources by 2020.[74]
>
> For Rio Tinto, the Net Positive Impact (NPI) goal means ensuring their actions have positive effects on biodiversity that balance as well as outweigh the inevitable negative effects from mining and mineral processing.[75]
>
> No Net Loss (NNL) for biodiversity[76] is the point at which impacts on biodiversity are balanced by measures taken to avoid and minimize them. This includes undertaking on-site restoration and finally offsetting any significant residual impacts on a suitable geographic scale, e.g. local, landscape-level, national, regional.

Rebooting business purpose and markets

Beyond sustainability, the definition of *business purpose* is shifting. The popular view that corporations exist principally for the purpose of Maximizing Shareholder Value (MSV) is increasingly questioned. In light of environmental concerns and trust issues following the 2007/2008 financial crash, concern is mounting over the unintended consequences associated with a business goal of MSV alone. These include short-term focused investment cycles, inequality, excessive executive pay and environmental externalities.[77] A 'New Cognitive Framework' for how business and governments see their relationship with natural and social capital and rethinking public good is needed.[78] A Sustainable Capitalism framework has been proposed by the Al Gore-supported Generation Management and Foundation,[79] which seeks to maximize long-term economic value creation by reforming markets to address real needs while considering all costs and stakeholders. At the societal level, Professor Tim O'Riordain proposes a transition to a society where well-being is the key focus and business purpose is beyond profit alone.

The world economy is on a dangerous cusp. Deflation is in the air and unemployment amongst the young is high. This is the ideal time to change course in favour of making wellbeing a central objective of economic, social and environmental policy coupled to public/private/voluntary initiatives for creating social value through sustainable enterprise. PROF. TIM O'RIORDAN OBE DL FBA, EMERITUS PROFESSOR OF ENVIRONMENTAL SCIENCES AT THE UNIVERSITY OF EAST ANGLIA AND NATURAL CAPITAL INITIATIVE ADVISORY BOARD

The Aldersgate Group (**www.aldersgategroup.org.uk**), a UK alliance of leaders from business, politics and civil society that drives action for a sustainable economy, has defined its ambition for an economy that properly recognizes natural and social capital alongside financial in An Economy That Works (**http://aneconomythatworks.org**). Success needs to be evident in six characteristics of the national economy: high employment, equality of access to opportunity, well-being as a core success measure, low carbon, zero waste and enhancing nature. To enable this Chairman Peter Young proposes:

Policies to enable these outcomes need to be long-term, inclusive, innovative and deliverable in a meaningful way at the community scale. Good places to start would be developing well-being to be as familiar and important as GDP to decision-makers; implementing a national natural capital strategy with an associated investment plan to begin to reverse the damage; and maintaining ambition and commitment to UK carbon targets through adherence to current, and adoption of future (5th), carbon budgets. PETER YOUNG, CHAIRMAN, THE ALDERSGATE GROUP

PART 4

Challenges, Opportunities and Next Steps

THIS CHAPTER OUTLINES THE KEY CHALLENGES and opportunities for integrating natural and social capital considerations in business decision-making with suggested next steps to watch. Key areas that must be addressed include:

- Mindset and lack of incentives

- Limitations in methods, data and tools

- Pros and cons of monetization

- Bridging the language and skills barriers across sustainability, financial and accounting communities.

Mindset and incentives

Short-termism and the singular profit maximization mindset at the core of capitalism is a major barrier for mainstreaming action at country and business levels to value and manage natural and social capital. The success of national economies and business are dominated by financial measures, for example, GDP/GNP, profit, revenues, earnings per share and cash flow. Wider non-financial measures of success, for example, societal well-being, resilient ecosystems and available resources are often not factored in. Short-termism dominating the market can undermine stability and long-term value creation efforts. Offering financial rewards for holding shares longer, for example, loyalty driven securities can motivate investors to take a longer-term view. Further, quarterly earnings results motivate businesses to manage for the short term and investors to focus on this as distinct from value creation over the long term. This is increasingly recognized with Unilever (**www.mc kinsey.com/features/capitalism/ paul_polman**) taking a lead. They have aligned management incentives for the long term and moved away from quarterly profit reporting.[80]

FIGURE 23.

SOURCE: Image from Bigstock, used under standard Content Usage Agreement.

Moving economic success factors 'Beyond GDP/GNP' to put natural and social capital on an equal footing with financial and other capitals is a key step to drive action. After this the financial systems, market pricing and incentive structures to enable this can more easily be put in place. Without incentives, regulatory and market, business action will remain in a small group of pioneering early adopters and not scale to the mainstream. In the words of one of these pioneers:

Instead of the goal of maximum linear growth in GDP, we should be thinking of maximum wellbeing for minimal planetary input. SIR IAN CHESHIRE, CEO, KINGFISHER GROUP PLC FROM *THE INDEPENDENT*, DECEMBER 2014[81]

At the business level, the financial accounting regulatory frameworks US GAAP set by the FASB and IFRS set by IASB, which regulate financial reporting requirements, for example, the balance sheet and profit and loss account, do not include natural and social capital considerations at present. While these include guidance on risk assessment and disclosure, natural and social capital is not yet a focus. This is a major gap in driving mainstream uptake. There is no mandatory incentive to measure, manage and report natural and social capital in annual business reports. This has been recognized for some time but action is still slow. Paul Hawkin, Amory and Hunter Lovins made this call to action as long ago as 1999 in the milestone book *Natural Capitalism*:

What would our economy look like if it fully valued all forms of capital, including human and natural capital? What if our economy were organized not around the lifeless abstractions of neoclassical economics and accountancy but biological realities of nature? What if Generally Accepted Accounting Principles booked natural and human capital not as a free amenity in punitive inexhaustible supply but as a finite and integrally valuable factor of production? NATURAL CAPITALISM, THE NEXT INDUSTRIAL REVOLUTION[82]

As standard methods are now evolving for natural and social capital accounting and valuation, seeking to include them in these financial accounting regulatory frameworks and associated guidance would incorporate the practices at source. This would enable scaling uptake in the mainstream much quicker than developing standards within the sustainability standards frameworks alone and where the current standards activity is starting.

Bridging barriers when worlds collide

As interest in natural and social capital grows, financial, accounting and sustainability professionals find their worlds colliding. These professionals operate in very different worlds in terms of language, motivations, skill sets and toolkits. Over the last 20 years the natural capital agenda has emerged from sustainability practitioners in NGOs, policy and research communities particularly. The engagement with business and particularly finance and accounting is a relatively recent phenomenon. At present sustainability and finance/accounting professionals are engaging which is excellent, and needed. However, this brings challenges. Quickly and effectively bridging the communication gaps and avoiding recreating the wheel on both sides is important to fast-tracking measurement and management of rapidly degrading natural capital.

The role of accountants and the CFO

The business case and mandate for integration of natural and social capital in decision-making within the finance and accounting professions is new and needs to be mainstreamed. A recent survey of 1,100 Chartered Global Management Accountants[83] identified lack of corporate mandate as the main reason for not reporting on sustainability. While the sustainability business case was generally accepted, 60 percent cited lack of demand from decision-makers and one third noted it was not part of their job. Other reasons included unavailable data or lack of knowledge/training as illustrated in Figure 24. However, more than two-thirds agreed that in the next few years their organizations will expect them to provide increasing amounts of environmental and social data. This is an area for accounting professionals to watch and prepare for.

FIGURE 24. Results from CGMA survey.

Survey question: What are your reasons for not including relevant Environmental and Social (ES) factors in the information and analysis you provide?

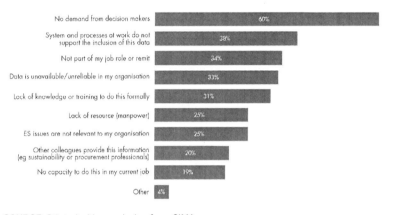

SOURCE: Printed with permission from CIMA

Studies from ACCA,[84] PWC[85] and the investor research institute[86] show sustainability, and particularly natural capital, is rarely included in financial reporting. This makes financial risks and opportunities from sustainability invisible in disclosure. As business and investors use financial materiality in the main to judge corporate performance, this gives a misleading impression. According to EY:

We remain locked in a paradigm dominated by a narrow view of financial, economic and shareholder value. Whilst things are starting to change, the real shift will only happen when a critical mass of business leaders demand and apply new ways to account for a broader perspective on value. STEVEN LANG, PARTNER, ERNST & YOUNG LLP

Accounting professional bodies increasingly see the management accountant's role as crucial with the challenge being to connect management accountants to the issue of sustainability and how it drives resilience for both society and organizations. They see a key role for management accountants in raising sustainability as a strategic issue, data gathering and integration in decision-making and reporting. While not traditionally associated with sustainability, accountants play an important role and are well positioned to connect natural capital risks and opportunities with financial performance. This can be promoted as a specialism within accountancy rather than the little known activity it is at present. CIMA make this case:

We need a big shift in mindset for organisations to adapt to the risks, and opportunities, that natural capital depletion presents. New corporate thinking needs to include the critical dependencies and impacts companies have on nature and link this to their business models. CFOs and accountants have an important role in facilitating this thinking. SANDRA RAPACIOLI, HEAD OF SUSTAINABILITY RESEARCH AND POLICY, CIMA

The CFOs' involvement in the business sustainability strategies is growing according to surveys by Accenture[87] and Deloitte. The Deloitte survey in 2013 found that 83 percent of CFOs were involved in setting their company's sustainability strategy. This was an increase from 65 percent in 2012.[88] For natural and social capital, CFO engagement is limited but growing. Initiatives such as the A4S CFOs Network are gathering a critical mass of early adopters to raise awareness and develop guidance in the language of finance. Engaging a busy CFO with many capital requests across the business on sustainability is a challenge Heads of Sustainability will understand. This is where financial valuation of natural and social capital provides an additional powerful engagement tool where the financials speak for themselves. The role of the CFO is key to effectively integrating natural and social capital considerations into the business and making the business case to the board. The case examples from The Crown Estate, M&S and United Utilities Group in Chapter 2 illustrate the importance of CFO leadership. Rachel Jackson at ACCA proposes that:

CFOs should utilize their senior position to raise awareness, educate and gain support of the board on material natural capital issues. These can then be integrated into key management and strategic decisions including risk assessments, as well as considering their inclusion in financial accounts. RACHEL JACKSON, HEAD OF SUSTAINABILITY, ACCA

Education

A key aspect of shifting mindsets and engaging finance professionals is ensuring sustainability is incorporated in education and capacity building. Sustainability needs to be a fundamental part of business finance and accounting training and certifications, such as MBA and chartered accounting accreditations. Sustainability is increasingly seen in innovative business degrees but still far from mainstream. Within business more generally, the recent *Skills for a sustainable economy: preparing for the perfect storm*[89] showed only 13 percent of over 950 companies surveyed were fully confident they have the skills to successfully compete in a sustainable economy.

Limitations in metrics and data

While valuation techniques exist and have been included in this book, the absence of formal standards and data systems that are accepted in the financial and sustainability communities is currently one feature limiting uptake. IFAC describes this challenge for business as follows:

Accounting for, and reporting on, natural capital has been hindered by the lack of a standard method to account for a capital that is in effect under shared ownership by society at large. A universal approach to natural capital accounting should help organizations to have confidence in measuring and valuing natural capital and to help them on their journey to be both transparent to the outside world and to drive their business decision-making. STATHIS GOULD, HEAD OF PAIB, INTERNATIONAL FEDERATION OF ACCOUNTANTS

Beyond this the current limitations and gaps in metrics and data to support mainstream integration of natural capital accounting and valuation in business include the following:

- A standardized suite of indicators are needed to enable business to understand their dependencies on natural and social capital. Indicators for measuring the direct environmental impacts of a business have well recognized standards, guides and tools. This is not the case for measuring use and dependency on ecosystem services and biodiversity. These also need to be consistent with classifications used in developing national accounting systems[90] to ensure performance benchmarks and progress tracking are meaningful in the future.

- Challenges with externality valuation and current techniques include technical limitations, relative results with large uncertainties and little robust data. Valuing biodiversity and ecosystem services using traditional environmental economic non market valuation techniques poses challenges that experts note reveal the limitations of these methods.[91] Also, at a business level, the large uncertainty and relative nature of externality estimates makes it difficult to meaningfully inform corporate accounting decisions. This is in comparison to environmental impacts data or internal costs which are absolute. Determining fit for purpose ways to value externalities for use in different business applications needs consideration in light of these challenges. For example, techniques for large landowners for site/landscape level applications are different from those informing product/supply chain decisions. A flexible framework that establishes a common language, scope and techniques suited for different business applications, which can be tested in early adopters, is needed.

- There are a range of databases that can inform natural capital assessments and a few for valuation (see Appendix on page 116). However, data gaps, inconsistent quality/reliability and inaccessibility for business use are challenges. At source, data are often poor, for example, for species and habitat values and differences across ecosystem services in world geographies add to the complexity. Recent natural capital data and monitoring system initiatives using remote sensing and satellite technology provide opportunities to leapfrog. Examples to watch include Microsoft's Global Ecosystems Model (GEM; http://research.microsoft.com/ en-us/projects/gef/), Google and WRI's Global Forest Watch (www. globalforestwatch.org), Natural Capital from Space (www.zsl.org/ science/indicators-and-assessments-unit) and Group on Earth Observations (www.earthobservations.org/geoss.php).

Pros and cons of monetization

A common criticism of financially valuing nature's services is that it will lead to commoditizing or privatizing nature. That is not the intent, however these unintended consequences need to be taken seriously as standard methods and accounting systems are developed and implemented. Care also needs to be taken to avoid an obsession with monetisation that leads to perfecting accounting practices and losing sight of the bigger picture rationale. The purpose of assigning a financial value is not to change the fundamental value of nature – which is arguably priceless – and many ecosystem services are irreplaceable. The importance of translating environmental and social impacts and dependencies information into financial information is that it allows more informed decision-making especially on trade-offs. This is more likely to result in action from key decision-makers who generally deal in financial terms, for example, CFOs. At the bigger picture level having a financial value for natural capital shared by society at large, as distinct from being perceived as 'free' can shift behaviour away from degradation to restoration.

Expectations should be managed on what valuation of externalities can achieve. Irrespective of trending sustainability sound bites that 'accountants will save the world', valuation and having accounting methods alone will not result in sustainable market transformation. There is also a 'so what' factor among some businesses who challenge whether adding a financial value beyond already knowing impacts and dependencies in physical terms, for example, tonnes of GHG emitted, tonnes of waste generated or metres^3/gallons of water used (or available for use) drives action any quicker. The financials should certainly help, but this remains to be seen. What is clear, is that without effective incentives – market or regulatory – to internalize these externalities action to drive enhancement of natural capital versus degradation will be slow.

In reality, environmental and social issues are too complex to be reduced to a financial value alone. Qualitative and quantitative information – non-financial and financial – is needed to understand the impacts and dependencies a company has on the planet. Beyond impacts and dependencies, wider issues, such as morals and business ethics, need to be considered. Different skills within the business, sustainability, governance and financial related, are required to assess these issues and determine suitable action. The critical issue is to integrate the non-financial and financial information and skills to enable effective decision-making that will enable long-term value creation for the business and the natural and social capital it depends on.

PART 5

Epilogue

IF YOU TAKE ONE MESSAGE AWAY FROM THIS BOOK it is the urgent financial rationale for reducing natural capital risk. Most of nature's services are not adequately captured in the market. The future shock for business is the potential for profit to be wiped out as natural capital is internalized through regulation and markets. Like the early adopters described in this book, companies who act now are better positioned to manage and thrive in a future 'resource-constrained' world.

The business case for integrating natural and social capital is clear in order to mitigate risk, secure resource supply, resilience, maintain a licence to operate, profit, reputation and ensure long-term value creation.

If you have been inspired to action in your business, take the next step. Raise awareness on the business case for integrating natural and social capital into decision-making and get commitment to measuring and managing this at board level. If you are the CFO or Head of Sustainability you have a key role to play in championing this business case and securing commitment.

In the words of the visionary HRH The Prince of Wales:

The ultimate bank on which we all depend – the bank of natural capital – is in the red; the debt is getting ever bigger and that is reducing Nature's resilience and considerably impeding her ability to re-stock. It leaves us dangerously exposed. HRH THE PRINCE OF WALES, SPEAKING AT THE PRINCE'S ACCOUNTING FOR SUSTAINABILITY FORUM, ST JAMES'S PALACE, LONDON, DECEMBER 2013[92]

Glossary

Association of Chartered Certified Accountants (ACCA)

Carbon Disclosure Standards Board (CDSB)

Chief Financial Officers (CFO)

Chartered Institute of Management Accountants (CIMA)

Cost–Benefit Analysis (CBA)

Environmental Management Accounting (EMA)

Environmental, Social and Governance (ESG)

Federal Accounting Standards Board (FASB)

Financial Institutions (FIs)

Full Cost Accounting (FCA)

Generally Accepted Accounting Principles (GAAP)

Global Reporting Initiative (GRI)

Greenhouse Gas emissions (GHG)

Integrated Reporting (<IR>)

International Accounting Standards Body (IASB)

International Financial Reporting Standards (IFRS)

Life Cycle Assessment (LCA)

Maximizing Shareholder Value (MSV)

Natural Capital Accounting (NCA)

Net Positive Impact (NPI)

Net Present Value (NPV)

No Net Loss (NNL)

Profit & Loss (P&L)

Replacement Cost Methodology (RCM)

Triple Bottom Line (TBL) Accounting

Triple Net Bottom Line (TNBL)

Willing To Pay (WTP)

Further Resources

- Accounting 4 Sustainability (A4S) CFO Leadership Network (**www. accountingforsustainability.org/cfos/network-of-chief-financial-officers**) and guides (www.accountingforsustainability.org/cfos/ **network-of-chief-financial-officers/a4s-cfo-leadership-network-activities**)

- Association of Chartered Certified Accountants (ACCA) and Sustainability (**www.accaglobal.com/uk/en/technical-activities/ sustainability.html**)

- BSR Ecosystem Services Business Group (**www.bsr.org/en/colla boration/groups/ecosystem-services-tools-markets**)

- Cambridge Program for Sustainability Leadership Natural Capital Leaders programme (**www.cisl.cam.ac.uk/business-action/natural -resource-security/natural-capital-leadership-compact**)

- CDP (**https://www.cdp.net**)

- Carbon Disclosure Standards Board (CDSB; **www.cdsb.net**) Climate Change Reporting Framework

- Chartered Institute of Management Accountants (CIMA) Accounting for Natural Capital: the Elephant in the Boardroom (**www.cima global.com/Thought-leadership/Research-topics/Sustainability/**

Accounting-for-natural-capital-the-elephant-in-the-boardroom/)

- Convention on Biological Diversity Global Platform on Business and Biodiversity (**www.cbd.int/business/**)

- EU Mapping and Assessment of Ecosystems and their Services in Europe (MAES; **http://ec.europa.eu/environment/nature/know ledge/ecosystem_assessment/index_en.htm**)

- Corporate Eco Forum Valuing Natural Capital Initiative (**www. corporateecoforum.com/valuing-natural-capital-initiative/**) report and Natural Capital Business Hub (**www.naturalcapitalhub.org**)

- EEU Business and Biodiversity Platform (B@B; **http://ec.europa. eu/environment/biodiversity/business/index_en.html**) platform draft NCA guide

- Global Reporting Initiative (**https://www.globalreporting.org/**) guidelines – G4 (**https://g4.globalreporting.org/**) version includes impacts and dependencies on natural resources as well as biodiversity values

- IPIECA (**www.ipieca.org/focus-area/biodiversity**) oil and gas industry association ecosystem service guidance: biodiversity and ecosystem services

- International Council on Mining and Metals (ICMM; **www.icmm. com/page/1182/good-practice-guidance-for-mining-and-bio diversity**) Mining and Biodiversity Good Practice Guidance

- IUCN Leaders for Nature (**www.leadersfornature.nl**) and TruePrice (**http://trueprice.org**) Dutch business initiatives

- Natural Capital Coalition (**www.naturalcapitalcoalition.org**) business case reports and Natural Capital Protocol project

- Natural Capital Financing Facility (**http://ec.europa.eu/environ ment/biodiversity/business/assets/pdf/ncff.pdf**)

- Natural Value Initiative (**www.naturalvalueinitiative.org**) on mining, energy, fisheries, pharmaceuticals and investors

- The Nature Conservancy (**www.nature.org/science-in-action/eco system-services.xml**) ecosystems and NatureVest (investors; **www.naturevesttnc.org/about.html**) programmes

- UK government National Ecosystems Assessment (**http://uknea. unep-wcmc.org**), Ecosystems Market Task Force (**https://www.gov. uk/government/groups/ecosystem-markets-task-force**) and Natural Capital Committee (**https://www.naturalcapitalcommittee.org**)

- UK Natural Capital Initiative (**www.naturalcapitalinitiative.org.uk**) and Valuing Nature Network (**www.valuing-nature.net**)

- UNEP Finance Initiative and Global Canopy Natural Capital Declaration (**www.naturalcapitaldeclaration.org**) for financial institutions to integrate natural capital in financial products and services

- UNEP TEEB (The Economics of Ecosystems and Biodiversity; **www. teebweb.org**)

- UN System of Environmental and Economic Accounts (SEEA; **www.wavespartnership.org/en**)

- WBCSD Redefining Value (**www.wbcsd.org/financialcapital.aspx**)

- Wealth Accounting and Valuation of Ecosystem Services (WAVES; **www.wavespartnership.org/en**)

- World Resource Institute (**www.wri.org/tags/ecosystem-services**) ecosystem services

- World Forum on Natural Capital (**www.naturalcapitalforum.com**) events organized by Scottish Wildlife and partners

- WWF Natural Capital project (**www.worldwildlife.org/projects/ the-natural-capital-project**)

Examples of guides and tools: natural capital assessment and valuation

- Co$ting Nature (**www.policysupport.org/costingnature**)

- CPSL Externality Valuation Assessment Tool (E.Valu.A.Te; **www.cisl. cam.ac.uk/business-action/natural-resource-security/natural- capital-leaders-platform#fragment-4**)

- EU Business and Biodiversity Platform Natural Capital Accounting for Business: Guide to Selecting an Approach (**http://ec.europa.eu/ environment/biodiversity/business/workstreams/Workstream1- Natural-Capital-Accounting/index_en.html**) and NCA Decision- matrix Tool (**www.cbd.int/business/**)

- Holcim and IUCN Biodiversity Indicator and Reporting System (BIRS)[93] to quantify the condition of habitats on their sites

- Natural Capital Project (**www.naturalcapitalproject.org**) Integrated Valuation of Environmental Services and Trade-offs (InVEST)

- KPMG True Value (**www.kpmg.com/global/en/topics/climate- change-sustainability-services/pages/a-new-vision-connecting- corporate.aspx**)

- PricewaterhouseCoopers (PwC) Total Impact Measurement & Management (TIMM; **www.pwc.com/totalimpact**)

- Earth Economics Simple Effective Resource for Valuing Ecosystem Services (SERVES; **www.esvaluation.org/serves.php**)

- Systain estell (**www.systain.com/en/applied-methodologies/estell/**)

- Trucost Natural Capital Analyzer (**www.trucost.com/naturalcapital analyzer**) and Water Risk Monetizer (**http://waterriskmonetizer. com/**)

- Truprice Consultation Draft Principles on methods for Impact Measurement and Valuation (**http://trueprice.org**)

- WRI WBCSD Guide to Corporate Ecosystem Valuation (CEV; **www. wbcsd.org/work-program/ecosystems/cev.aspx**) and WBCSD Guide to Water Valuation (**www.wbcsd.org/Pages/EDocument/ EDocumentDetails.aspx?ID=15801&NoSearchContextKey=true**)

Database examples

- World Conservation Monitoring Centre (UNEP-WCMC) databases, for example, World Database on Protected Areas, species database and datasets, tools (**www.protectedplanet.net**)

- The Food and Agricultural Organisation (FAO) databases, for example, FAO Aquastat Database (**www.fao.org/nr/gaez/about-data-portal/en/**)

- IUCN's knowledge products, for example, IUCN Red List of Threatened Species™ (**www.iucnredlist.org**)

- Earth Economics: Ecosystem Valuation Toolkit (EVT; http://esvaluation.org)

- Ecosystem Service Valuation database (ESVD; www.es-partnership.org/esp/80763/5/0/50)

- Environmental Valuation Reference Inventory (EVRI; https://www.evri.ca/Global/Splash.aspx)

Notes and References

1. CIMA. 2013. *Accounting for Natural Capital – The Elephant in the Boardroom*, CIMA, EY, IFAC, Natural Capital Coalition,http://www.cimaglobal.com/Thought-leadership/Research-topics/Sustainability/Accounting-for-natural-capital-the-elephant-in-the-boardroom/

2. Figures are for 2010 and from sources: Costanza, R. et al., World Bank, Earth Policy Institute as per A4S and Information is Beautiful Studio, *Costing the Earth*, https://www.accountingforsustainability.org/forum-event/the-economic-invisibility-of-nature. There is debate on the economic value of ecosystem services as the total economic value provided by nature's services to the global economy is difficult to determine and has high uncertainties. Costanza, R. et al. 1997. The value of the world's ecosystem services and natural capital. *Nature* (Vol. 387, 15 May), http://www.esd.ornl.gov/benefits_conference/nature_paper.pdf estimated a range of $16–54 trillion and average of $33 trillion worth of ecosystem services per year (1995). An updated study from Costanza, R. et al. 2014. Changes in the global value of ecosystem services. *Global Environmental Change* (Volume 26, May): 152–158, http://www.sciencedirect.com/science/article/pii/S0959378014000685) increased this estimate to US$125 trillion/year (2011) (with the estimated loss of ecosystem services from 1997 to 2011 due to land use change being valued at $20.2 trillion/yr, using the updated values). UNEP. 2012. *Dead planet, living planet: Biodiversity and ecosystem restoration for sustainable development, http://www.unep.org/pdf/RRAecosystems_screen.pdf* estimates it to be $72 trillion/year. Regarding preservation costs, the UN estimates $300 billion as the cost of sustainable management of agriculture, forests, freshwater and coastal and marine ecosystems. *Source*: Reuters, 8 March 2012, *Saving biodiversity: a $300 billion-a-year challenge*, http://www.timeslive.co.za/scitech/2012/03/08/saving-biodiversity-a-300-billion-a-year-challenge

3. UNEP. 2012. *Dead Planet, Living Planet Biodiversity And Ecosystem Restoration For Sustainable Development,* **http://www.unep.org/pdf/RRAecosystems_screen.pdf**

4. UNPRI. 2010. *Putting a Price on Global Environmental Damage,* UNPRI, UNEP FI and Trucost, October.

5. UNPRI. 2010. *Putting a Price on Global Environmental Damage,* UNPRI, UNEP FI and Trucost, October.

6. Trucost. 2013. *Natural Capital at Risk Top 100 Externalities of Business,* for Natural Capital Coalition (**www.naturalcapitalcoalition.org**). Sectors analysed were primary production (agriculture, forestry, fisheries, mining, oil and gas exploration, utilities) and primary processing (cement, steel, pulp and paper, petrochemicals).

7. UNEP. 2012. *Fifth Global Environment Outlook,* 2012, **http://www.unep.org/geo/**

8. UNEP. *TEEB* www.teebtest.org

9. KPMG and NVI. 2011. *Biodiversity and ecosystem services: Risk and opportunity analysis within the pharmaceutical sector,* **http://www.naturalvalueinitiative.org/download/documents/Publications/Biodiversity%20and%20Ecosystem%20Services%20report%20July%202011.pdf**

10. Defined by the IIRC. 2013. Integrated Reporting Framework **http://www.theiirc.org/international-ir-framework/**

11. Unilever. 2012. Sustainable Living GHG emissions **http://www.unilever.com/images/PDF_generator_-_Greenhouse_gases_tcm_13-365028.pdf**

12. A survey of 26 businesses across nine sectors identified freshwater, renewable energy, climate regulation and available productive land as the most important natural capital business risks in the next three to five years. Sectors included food & agribusiness, chemicals, mining & construction, electric utility, oil & gas, apparel, water & waste management, packaging and financial/professional

services. Over 75% of the companies surveyed had over US$1 billion in annual revenues. *Source*: Innovastat. 2013. *Organisational Change for Natural Capital Management* , Natural Capital Coalition, http://**www.naturalcapitalcoalition.org**

13. Kering Group Environmental Profit & Loss, **http://www.kering.com/en/ sustainability/environmental-pl**

14. Harvard *Business Review. 2013. The big idea: The sustai*nable economy. *Harvard Business Review,* **https://hbr.org/2011/10/the-sustainable-economy/ar/1**

15. Esty, D. and Simmons, P. 2011. *The Green to Gold Business Playbook: How to Implement Sustainability Practices for Bottom-Line Results in Every Business Function* (Hoboken, NJ: Wiley).

16. Tercek, M. 2013. *Nature's Fortune: How Business and Society Thrive By Investing in Nature,* **http://www.marktercek.com/natures-fortune/**

17. University of Oxford and Arabesque Partners, September 2014. *From the Stockholder to the Stakeholder: How sustainability can drive financial outperformance,* **http://arabesque.com/**

18. Quote from page 6, University of Oxford and Arabesque Partners, September 2014, *From the Stockholder to the Stakeholder: How sustainability can drive financial outperformance,* **http://arabesque.com/**

19. Ecceles, R. et al. 2012. Harvard Business School and London Business School, May, *The Impact of a Corporate Culture of Sustainability on Corporate Behavior and Performance,* **http://hbswk.hbs.edu/item/6865.html**

20. Bloomberg Carbon Risk Valuation Tool (CRVT), **http://about.bnef.com/white-papers/bloomberg-carbon-risk-valuation-tool-2/**

21. B4B, **http://www.equator-principles.com/index.php/best-practice-resources/ B4B**

22. Credit Suisse, WWF, ESG Banks *Guide, 2014.* **http://assets.panda.org/ downloads/wwf_environmental_social_governance_banks_guide_report.pdf**

23. Credit Suisse, McKinsey, WWF, 2014. *Conservation Finance, Moving beyond*

donor funding toward an investor-driven approach https://www.credit-suisse. com/media/production/cc/docs/responsibility/conservation-finance-en. pdf?WT.i_short-url=%2Fresponsibility%2Fdoc%2Fconservation_finance_ en.pdf&WT.i_target_url=%2Fmedia%2Fproduction%2Fcc%2Fdocs%2Frespon sibility%2Fconservation-finance-en.pdf

24. IDB. 2012. www.iadb.org/biodiversityLAC

25. Definitions of ecosystem services are based on UN Millennium Ecosystem Assessment. 2005. Ecosystems and Human Wellbeing: *Synthesis (Washington, DC: Island Press),* www.maweb.org and Common International Classification of Ecosystem Services, 2012, http://www.cices.eu/

26. Formally called 'social and relationship' capital according to the IIRC, Integrated Reporting Framework, http://www.theiirc.org/international-ir-framework/

27. WWF International. 2014. *Living Planet Report 2014 Species and Spaces, People and Places* (Water Footprint Network with WWF, Zoological Society of London and Global Footprint Network), ISBN 978-2-940443-87-1 , http://wwf. panda.org/about_our_earth/all_publications/living_planet_report/

28. UN. 2005. Millennium Ecosystem Assessment. *Ecosystems and Human Wellbeing: Synthesis* (Washington, DC: Island Press), www.maweb.org.

29. WWF International. 2014. *Living Planet Report 2014 Species and Spaces, People and Places* (Water Footprint Network with WWF, Zoological Society of London and Global Footprint Network), ISBN 978-2-940443-87-1 , http://wwf. panda.org/about_our_earth/all_publications/living_planet_report/

30. Innovastat. 2013. *Organisational Change for Natural Capital Management* for Natural Capital Coalition, 2013, http://www.naturalcapitalcoalition.org

31. A set of nine planetary boundaries have been quantified. Crossing these boundaries could generate abrupt or irreversible environmental change based on Stockholm Resilience Centre. 2009. *Planetary Boundaries model,* http://www. stockholmresilience.org/21/research/research-programmes/planetary- boundaries.html and Steffen, W. et al. 2015. Planetary boundaries: Guiding

human development on a changing planet. *Science* (January), DOI: 10.1126/science.1259855, http://www.sciencemag.org/content/early/2015/01/14/science.1259855

32. *New York Times*. May 2007. Climate change puts nuclear energy in hot water, http://www.nytimes.com/2007/05/20/health/20iht-nuke.1.5788480.html?pagewanted=all&_r=1&

33. Waage, S. 2014. T*he 'Laws' of Investment: Sunset of the Era of Moore's Law & the Dawn of Diamond's Law?*, http://www.economistinsights.com/sustainability-resources/opinion/%E2%80%98laws%E2%80%99-investment

34. WEF. 2015. *Global Risks*, http://reports.weforum.org/global-risks-2015/

35. McKinsey. 2013. *Resource Revolution*, http://www.mckinsey.com/insights/energy_resources_materials/resource_revolution_tracking_global_commodity_markets

36. Costanza, R. et al. 1997. The value of the world's ecosystem services and natural capital. *Nature* (Volume 387, 15 May), http://www.esd.ornl.gov/benefits_conference/nature_paper.pdf

37. Economy for the Common Good, Common Good Balance Sheets, https://www.ecogood.org/en

38. CGMA. 2014. CGMA® Report: *How management accountants drive sustainable corporate strategies*, CGMA (AICPA and CIMA) and A4S, December.

39. CGMA. 2014. G*lobal Management Accounting Principles* © October.

40. US Generally Accepted Accounting Principles, http://www.fasb.org/home

41. International Financial Reporting Standards, http://www.ifrs.org/IFRSs/Pages/IFRS.aspx

42. The Security and Exchange Commission is looking to switch from US GAAP to IFRS by 2015

43. LCA Environmental indicators are defined in standards e.g. ISO 14040/44

Life Cycle Assessment http://www.iso.org/iso/home/store/catalogue_tc/catalogue_tc_browse.htm?commid=54854, EU Product or Organisational Environmental Footprint (PEF) Guide, http://ec.europa.eu/environment/eussd/smgp/index.htm

44. UNEP SETAC. 2011. Guidelines For Social Life Cycle Assessment of Products, http://www.unep.fr/shared/publications/pdf/DTIx1164xPA-guidelines_sLCA. pdf

45. Maxwell, D. and McKenzie, E. 2014. *Valuing Nature in Business*: **Towards a Harmonized Framework & Taking Stock**, Natural Capital Coalition, ICAEW, May 2014, http://www.naturalcapitalcoalition.org. These publications provide a comprehensive resource collating and summarizing current natural capital initiatives.

46. For more information see http://www.patagonia.com/us/patagonia.go?assetid=100742 and video https://www.youtube.com/watch?v=Jt3O4v-v3tU

47. IFAC. 2005. *International Guidance Document: Environmental Management Accounting,* http://www.ifac.org/publications-resources/international-guidance-document-environmental-management-accounting

48. Steen, B. 2005. Environmental costs and benefits in life cycle costing. Management of Environmental Quality (Volume 16, Number 2): 107–118, http://publications.lib.chalmers.se/publication/7169

49. Swarr, T. et al. 2011. Environm*ental Life Cycle Costing: A Code of Practice. SETAC,* https://www.setac.org/store/ViewProduct.aspx?id=1033860

50. Barbier, E. 2012. Ecosystem services and wealth accounting. In UNU-IHDP and UNEP. *Inclusive Wealth Report 2012. Measuring Progress toward Sustainability* (Cambridge: Cambridge University Press), http://inclusivewealthindex.org/ch-8-2012/

51. DiMuro, J.L. et al. 2014. **A financial and environmental analysis of constructed wetlands for industrial wastewater treatment.** Journal of Industrial Ecology, pages 631–640, Article first published online: 18 April 2014, DOI: 10.1111/jiec.12129, http://onlinelibrary.wiley.com/doi/10.1111/jiec.12129/abstract

52. Bateman, I. et al. 2013. Bringing ecosystem services into economic decision-making: Land use in the United Kingdom. Science (Volume 341): 45.

53. Maxwell, D. and McKenzie, E. 2014. *Valuing Nature in Business*: **Towards a Harmonized Framework & Taking Stock**, Natural Capital Coalition, ICAEW, May 2014, http://**www.naturalcapitalcoalition.org**

54. BSR. 2015. Making the Invisible Visible: Analytical Tools for Assessing Business Impacts & Dependencies Upon Ecosystem Services, January 2015 update, **http://www.bsr.org/reports/BSR_Analytical_Tools_for_Ecosystem_Services_2015.pdf**

55. UNEP, TEEB, **http://www.teebweb.org/**

56. Corporate Eco Forum, **The New Business Imperative-Valuing Natural Capital**

57. EU Commission's Business and Biodiversity Platform, 2015, *Natural Capital Accounting for Business: Guide to Selecting an Approach* and *NCA Decision-matrix Tool*, **http://ec.europa.eu/environment/biodiversity/business/workstreams/ Workstream1-Natural-Capital-Accounting/index_en.html**

58. Natural Capital Committee, 2015, *Developing Corporate Natural Capital Accounts Guidelines*, EFTEC, RSPB, PWC, Jan 2015, **https://www.natural capitalcommittee.org/corporate-natural-capital-accounting.html**

59. SEEA Briefing Notes: Measurement Framework in Support of Sustainable Development and Green Economy Policy; SEEA Experimental Ecosystem Accounting; SEEA-Water: Monitoring Framework for Water, **http://unstats. un.org/unsd/envaccounting/seea.asp**

60. WAVES, **http://www.wavespartnership.org/en**

61. BBOP, *Business Biodiversity Offset Standard*, **http://bbop.forest-trends.org/**

62. UN REDD, **http://www.un-redd.org**

63. OECD. 2010. *Paying for Biodiversity: Enhancing the Cost-effectiveness of Payments for Ecosystem Services* (Paris: OECD).

64. Latin American Water Funds Partnership, **http://www.femsa.com/en/actions-with-value/latin-american-water-fund-partnership**

65. Smith, S. et al. 2013. *Payments for Ecosystem Services: A Best Practice Guide* (London: Defra), **https://www.gov.uk/government/uploads/system/uploads/ attachment_data/file/200920/pb13932-pes-bestpractice-20130522.pdf**

66. Bennett, G., and N. Carroll. 2014. *Gaining Depth: State of Watershed Investment 2014*, p.3., **http://www.ecosystemmarketplace.com/reports/sowi201**

67. Ioannou, I and Serafeim, G. The Consequences of Mandatory Corporate Sustainability Reporting: Evidence from Four Countries. Working paper, Harvard Business Review, **http://www.hbs.edu/faculty/Publication%20Files/11-100_ 7f383b79-8dad-462d-90df-324e298acb49.pdf**

68. Eco-Business, 17 October 2014. *SGX to make sustainability reporting mandatory*, **http://www.eco-business.com/news/sgx-make-sustainability-reporting- mandatory/**

69. European Commission. 2014. *Directive 2013/34/EU on non-financial reporting*, **http://eur-lex.europa.eu/LexUriServ/LexUriServ.do?uri=OJ:L:2013: 182:0019:0076:EN:PDF**

70. IFC, *Environmental and Social Performance Standards* **http://www.ifc.org/ wps/wcm/connect/topics_ext_content/ifc_external_corporate_site/ifc+ sustainability/our+approach/risk+management/performance+standards/ environmental+and+social+performance+standards+and+guidance+notes**

71. SASB, **http://www.sasb.org/**

72. Global Investors Statement on Climate Change, **http://investorsonclimate change.org/**. Partners include Asia Investor Group on Climate Change (AIGCC), Institutional Investors Group on Climate Change (IIGCC), Ceres Investor Network on Climate Risk (INCR) and Investor Group on Climate Change Australia/New Zealand (IGCC).

73. Based on the <IR> Framework, IIRC,2013, Integrated Reporting Framework **http://www.theiirc.org/international-ir-framework/**

74. Kingfisher Group plc, Net Positive, **http://www.kingfisher.com/netpositive/ index.asp?pageid=1**

75. Rio Tinto and IUCN,, Exploring *ecosystem valuation to move towards a Net Positive Impact on biodiversity in the mining sector (2011) and Forecasting the path towards a Net Positive Impact on biodiversity for Rio Tinto QMM (2012)* http://www.iucn.org/knowledge/publications_doc/publications/?8922/Exploring-ecosystem-valuation-to-move-towards-net-positive-impact-on-biodiversity-in-the-mining-sector

76. IFC. 2012. Performance Standard 6 Biodiversity Conservation and Sustainable Management of Living Natural Resources, http://www.ifc.org/wps/wcm/connect/topics_ext_content/ifc_external_corporate_site/ifc+sustainability/our+approach/risk+management/performance+standards/environmental+and+social+performance+standards+and+guidance+notes

77. Purpose of the Corporation Project, 2014, http://www.purposeofcorporation.org/"

78. Sainty, R. 2012. Valuing natural capital needs a new mindset. *Ethical Investor*, http://ethicalinvestor.com.au/valuing-natural-capital-needs-a-new-mindset/

79. Generation Foundation. 2012. *Sustainable Capitalism White Paper,* http://genfound.org/initiatives/

80. McKinsey, Paul Polman interview Unilever, http://www.mckinsey.com/features/capitalism/paul_polman

81. *Independent*. 2014. Sir Ian Cheshire: Seeing the big picture on sustainable growth will rescue our economy, society and environment, http://www.independent.co.uk/news/business/comment/sir-ian-cheshire-seeing-the-big-picture-on-sustainable-growth-will-rescue-our-economy-society-and-environment-9911407.html

82. Hawkin, P. Lovins, A. and Lovins, H. 1999. *Natural Capitalism, The Next Industrial Revolution* (London: Earthscan), http://www.natcap.org/

83. CGMA. 2014. CGMA® Report: *How management accountants drive sustainable corporate strategies*, CGMA (AICPA and CIMA) and A4S, December, http://www.cgma.org/Resources/Reports/DownloadableDocuments/Redressing-the-balance.pdf

84. ACCA, KPMG and Flora and Fauna International. 2012. *Is natural capital a material issue? An evaluation of the relevance of biodiversity, and ecosystem services to accountancy professionals and the private sector,* http://www.accaglobal.com/content/dam/acca/global/PDF-technical/environmental-publications/natural-capital.pdf

85. 'Biodiversity threat will eclipse climate change economic impacts but still misses CEO and valuations radar – PwC study', PwC, 22 May 2010, http://pwc.blogs.com/press_room/2010/05/biodiversity-threat-will-eclipse-climate-change-economic-impacts-but-still-misses-ceo-and-valuations.html

86. Investor Responsibility Research Center Institute. 2013. *Integrated Financial and Sustainability Reporting in the United States,* http://irrcinstitute.org/news/first-comprehensive-study-on-state-of-integrated-reporting-in-united-states_pr_04_29_2013.php

87. CIMA and Accenture. 2011. *Sustainability Performance Management, How CFOs can unlock value.*

88. Deloitte. 2013. *CFOs and Sustainability: Shaping their roles in an evolving environment,* http://www2.deloitte.com/content/dam/Deloitte/us/Documents/risk/us-aers-imo-deloitte-cfos-sustainability-08122014.pdf

89. IEMA. 2014. *Skills for a sustainable economy: preparing for the perfect storm,* Institute of Environmental Management and Assessment.

90. E.g. Common International Classification of Ecosystem Services (CICES) which is informing the UN System of Environmental Economic Accounts – http://cices.eu/

91. Atkinson, G. et al. 2014. Valuing ecosystem services and biodiversity. In Helm, D. and Hepburn, C. (eds) *Nature in the Balance, The Economics of Biodiversity* (Oxford: Oxford University Press), http://ukcatalogue.oup.com/product/9780199676880.do

92. HRH The Prince of Wales speech at A4SForum, 2013 http://www.accountingforsustainability.org/a4s-forum-event-2013

93. Imboden, C. et al. 2014. B*iodiversity Indicator and Reporting System (BIRS): Proposal for a Habitat Based Biodiversity Monitoring System at Holcim Sites (Gland, Switzerland: IUCN),* **http://www.holcim.com/fileadmin/templates/ CORP/doc/SD/BIRS_recommendations.pdf**

Lightning Source UK Ltd.
Milton Keynes UK
UKOW04f1233300415

250658UK00002B/26/P

9 781910 174449